Of Golden Toads and Serpents' Roads

NUMBER THIRTY-FOUR
Louise Lindsey Merrick Natural Environment Series

Of Golden Toads
and

Serpents' Roads

PAUL FREED

Texas A&M University Press   •   College Station

Library of Congress Cataloging-in-Publication Data

Freed, Paul, 1955–
        Of golden toads and serpents' roads / Paul Freed.—1st ed.
            p. cm.—(Louise Lindsey Merrick natural environment
    series no. 34)
        ISBN 1-58544-248-8 (cloth : alk. paper)—
        ISBN 1-58544-271-2 (pbk. : alk. paper)
        1. Reptiles—Collection and preservation.   2. Amphibians—
    Collection and preservation.   3. Freed, Paul, 1955—Journeys.
    I. Title.   II. Series.
    QL645.65.F74   2003
    597.9'092—dc21   2003000552

Grants from the
East Texas Herpetological Society
and the Houston Zoo
helped make the publication of this book possible.

To colleagues,
friends,
and loved ones,
past and present,
and especially
to the memory of
my father-in-law,
Al Lester,
a kind, gentle,
and devoted family man
who taught me that
"Everything is relative."

● ●

Contents

Foreword

Buyers of this book will read it with remembrances and pleasure. Like most field biologists, I have "been there and done that" but failed to put it into words. Paul Freed has accomplished our task for us in a very eloquent manner.

Those of us who have suffered hardships chasing critters in the pursuit of knowledge, or who have a flair for photography of wild creatures, have empathy for Paul. Who among field biologists has not contracted beefworms, dysentery, and a sundry of diseases, both tropical and non-tropical, or suffered insect bites, spider bites, snake bites, vehicle breakdowns, floods, broiling sun, things stolen, bribes, and export (and import) permit problems?

Paul writes with great fervor, and the reader can feel the joy, disappointment, and candor of every moment. Like Paul, many of us have a love of the tropics that transcends comprehension. We go there to dwell in what we consider to be the essence of the animal and plant world. We are almost mindless in our desire to capture the feeling of God's world, unaltered, unfathomable, mysterious, and ever changing. Paul has captured these moments, holds them before us, and lets us see them again in our own eyes. Thanks, Paul, for a job well done.

James R. Dixon

Preface

As an avid student of herpetology, I began my adventures by traveling extensively throughout the United States. I was searching for the unusual as well as the common species of native reptiles and amphibians. Fifteen years later, I found myself wanting more: additional challenges, more excitement—and ultimately succumbing to the allure of exotic lands. I decided it was time to raise the bar to much greater heights. I knew this would be an expensive habit, but I was confident I could handle it; I believed that I could quit anytime I wanted, but I was wrong. Thus I began to feed my insatiable hunger for world travel—a hunger that has kept me on the brink of poverty and made many travel agents rich.

International travel can be fraught with problems. A common dilemma faced by many amateur adventurers is deciding where to go. With scores of countries to choose from, travelers can visit locations with an enormous diversity of habitats, flora, fauna, and, of course, people. So how does one decide where paradise lies? Perhaps a television documentary about a specific country or group of animals is what stirs one's interest, or maybe it is an article in a nature magazine or book. Even a firsthand account from a friend or acquaintance who has already made such a trip can influence one's decision. All of the above have at one time or another helped me to decide where I might go.

But then, it is often easier to decide where not to go. Since my main interest is herpetology, I logically eliminated from consideration the polar ice caps (that is, Antarctica), where cold-blooded creatures are absent. I also struck out countries that were politically unstable or openly hostile, as well as those that were largely inaccessible or would have excessively high costs. Even when omitting these few exceptions, there are still many exciting destinations, both near and far, from which to choose.

After each trip, friends and colleagues often approach me to show and tell of my recent adventures. These requests usually culminate in a kind of ritualistic slide show, during which I present a travelogue in an attempt to dazzle the gathered masses. Naturally, I try to show only the slides that best convey images of beauty, instill in the viewers a sense of awe, or tell stories of great success. However, there is really no "perfect" trip. There always seem to be unforeseen circumstances that demand compromise and sacrifice. By anticipating such potential problems, travelers are better able to make the necessary adjustments when disaster strikes.

What most people see when they attend one of my presentations is a polished and refined end product. This usually leads to comments such as, "That looked like fun; can I go with you next time?" or "It looks like you had a nice vacation." They do not realize that such trips are anything *but* a vacation. Fun and excitement are usually a result but not without an overwhelming amount of hard work. The underlying purpose of these trips is research, more specifically, herpetological parasitology, a study that requires collecting live reptiles and amphibians. Collecting and exporting permits are exceedingly time consuming to obtain, taking anywhere from six months to a year (when they are possible to obtain at all).

My beginnings as a professional scientist arose in a museum setting. The people who work in museums view wildlife very differently than those who work with animals in other biological fields such as zoos, veterinary medicine, or even within the pet industry. In order to study and understand the behavior of an animal, one must observe it under many varied conditions. In contrast, museum work is not about studying living animals that reveal their attributes by actions but is about studying preserved specimens, internally and externally, to learn what otherwise cannot be gleaned from a living animal. Therefore, these preserved specimens are relegated to these "afterlife" repositories where researchers have access to them. Despite the apparent morbidity of the subject, the work of museums is extremely necessary for the further development of our understanding of all wildlife.

During my herpetological research studies, I have adopted both zoo and museum ideologies to form the premise of my research; that is, I have incorporated two seemingly disjunct disciplines: the protection and "preservation" of wildlife. I collected animals and kept them alive for parasitological and behavioral observations; many of the animals I collected have lived more than ten years under captive conditions. Upon their natural deaths, however, I preserved them and donated them to appropriate museums.

Some may argue that far too many animals have been sacrificed in the name of science only to end up in jars in some dusty, old museum. There are two important factors concerning these animals that most people are probably not aware of. The first of which is that not all of the preserved specimens housed by museums are killed by museum researchers. Many are acquired after finding them already dead on roads. Others are often donated to museums upon the completion of field studies, classroom use, or their natural demise in zoos, laboratories, or universities.

The other important issue involves the concept of numbers. Adding up all the preserved specimens in all the museums worldwide results in a smaller number than that of animals tragically killed *each* year by vehicular traffic, wanton abuse by people, or by natural disasters such as floods, storms, or wildfires. And, what is more, those preserved specimens often last well over one hundred years, thereby allowing generations of researchers to study, learn, and benefit from these animals again and again.

• •

Wildlife biology is in a constant state of flux. As a result, researchers, taxonomists, and herpetologists are forever changing, updating, and revising the scientific names associated with animals. Many of the species I encountered during my trips have been subject to several nomenclature changes since I first observed and/or collected them. For the sake of thoroughness, I have listed the currently accepted scientific name of each species mentioned, but I have also included (in brackets [ ]) the scientific name of that animal at the time of my observation. Whenever possible, common names have been used, but for some no standardized ones exist, so I have included a scientific name for clarity.

In the following pages, I try to share some of my international travel experiences—the successful ones and those not so successful. Ultimately, my purpose for writing this book is to illustrate, sometimes in a humorous way, that despite some obstacles and disappointments, anyone can experience the exhilaration of international travel and the exciting world of nature.

Acknowledgments

For their assistance in the field, my thanks go to Denis Achu, Deborah Burdick, Angelo Capparella, Tom Dale, Hartwig Berger Dell'mour, Vickie Fowler, Joe Furman, Mike Griffin, George Hagnauer, Gary Migues, Phillippe Morelet, John O'Neill, and Mike Sharp. For reading and reviewing the manuscript and for providing numerous insights and improvements, I thank Evelyn Farr, Nancy Greig, Lisa Hooten, William W. Lamar, Charles Mann, Pat Tovsen, and Jerry Walls. I am also indebted to two reviewers, Dr. James R. Dixon and Dr. Eric R. Pianka, both of whom added substantial details and information to the text, specifically in terms of the natural history of the exotic wildlife. I would like to express many thanks to the administrative staff at the Houston Zoological Gardens for allowing my frequent and lengthy departures from work and for kindly accepting and caring for the exotic specimens I brought back with me from my various trips. The staff in all sections of the Carnegie Museum of Natural History have helped me throughout my travels for the past twenty years, and to all of them I give my sincerest thanks. To the Texas A&M University Press staff, whose keen eyes in detecting all my many imperfections and mistakes eventually turned a diamond in the rough into a readable text, I offer my deepest appreciation. Special thanks go to John Werler and John and Gloria Tveten, who, among the three of them, spent more time and effort reading, editing, and rewriting the text than I did. (Despite all the help I received, any and all errors, mistakes, or omissions are mine alone.)

To my mentor, co-worker, and colleague, the late Jack McCoy, I extend my deepest gratitude for his patience, his teachings, and most of all his friendship. Finally, to my wife Barbara, I would like to express my sincerest gratitude for her love, support, guidance, and encouragement, without which this book would never have been written.

••

Grants from the East Texas Herpetological Society and the Houston Zoo helped make the publication of this book possible.

Of Golden Toads and Serpents' Roads

CHAPTER 1

Costa Rica

Of Golden Toads

AT TWENTY-FIVE MILES AN HOUR, one blacktop road looks
pretty much like any other, but there are exceptions. This road was clearly
one of the exceptions. Unlike the state, county, and secondary roads I had
traveled endlessly throughout Texas, Nevada, and Arizona and across the
eastern seaboard, this one was special—special, because no matter what I
might find, and no matter what might lie ahead, it would undoubtedly
leave me with an impression that time itself could not erase. The fact that
I was now here when just yesterday I had been fighting the daily drudgery
of Houston city traffic was in itself a milestone.

The myriad sounds that were part of my regular nightly routine back
home—the rhythmic staccato-like chirping of crickets and the harmo-
nizing clicks, grunts, and trills of amorous anurans (frogs and toads) court-
ing in roadside ditches—now seemed distant and obscure. Here, I had
transcended the highways and back roads of my hometown haunts, passing up that "special" road where friends would gather to find the ordinary and the mundane. I was far from that now, both in distance and in
professional stature. I was finally in the big leagues.

It was just after 9:00 P.M.; a light rain had fallen all night. As I hunched
over the steering wheel, my knuckles were white from the tight grip I used
to guide the vehicle. I was completely mesmerized by the approaching

pavement ahead of me. Afraid to blink, I let my eyes dart back and forth over the road. The suspense was killing me. What would it be—a frog, a toad, maybe the jackpot, a snake? I kept recalling the advice that several colleagues had emphasized before my departure: Road collecting is unproductive because few animals are found on the well-traveled pavements. Perhaps they were right. It had been almost half an hour and I had yet to see a thing. But why? If road cruising works in the United States, why wouldn't it work here? After all, the principle should be the same wherever you go. You just drive slowly and allow your headlights to pick up the reflection of an animal in the road. Then, jump out of the car (remembering to stop first) and bag your catch. Sounds simple enough, but there are some drawbacks associated with this technique. Often there is no place to pull off the road, or there may be vehicular traffic in front of or behind you. Sometimes the animal moves quickly and gets off the road before you can stop to retrieve it. None of that had happened tonight, and I felt confident it would be only a matter of time before I made my first catch.

It was about 9:45 P.M. when I saw something crossing the road ahead of me. Slamming on the brakes, I flew out of the car. Shining my flashlight on the object I gasped, "That's not possible; those are not found in the wild." Stretched out at my feet was a two-foot-long baby boa constrictor. Until now, I had always thought these animals, like gerbils and parrots, were found only in pet shops. After a brief celebratory dance, I photographed the prize to document my unbelievably rare find. Actually, I would no longer call it rare, because by the end of the night I had collected fourteen additional snakes (including four more baby boas) and several dozen frogs and toads. So much for the so-called experts' claim that you cannot find animals by road cruising in Costa Rica.

By 2:30 A.M., with my head rested against the rock-hard ground that was to be my pillow for the weeks that followed, I knew I had started something I would never be able to satisfy completely, but that I would be willing to spend the rest of my life trying.

••

So began my first experience at international herp collecting, and it was not as easy as just getting on a plane, landing in a foreign country, and collecting wildlife. A great deal of planning and preparation went into this and subsequent trips.

I had chosen Costa Rica for many reasons. It was relatively close to the United States, a major consideration when you are not rich and most of your travel budget is consumed by airfare. Furthermore, a considerable number of my friends and colleagues had been to Costa Rica and were all mesmerized by its beauty and diverse wildlife. But what most influenced my decision to visit this country came from the television nature shows I had seen about Costa Rica. These, combined with the numerous articles and pictorials that vividly depicted so many of this country's rich and often unique flora and fauna, helped me to confirm that decision.

Back in the 1950s and 1960s, anyone could travel to a foreign country and indiscriminately bag every conceivable kind of wild-caught animal. This reckless behavior has fortunately long since ended. Today, if you wish to collect wildlife or plants in a foreign country (or even in the United States, for that matter), you are required to produce lengthy proposals—usually based on some kind of scientific research—to justify your wants. The restriction is in large part due to the enormous quantities of animals that have been exported from these countries. In the past, some countries allowed the export of hundreds of thousands of animals from their borders in a single year. To prevent this wholesale exploitation, which if left unchecked could lead to severe localized depletions, many countries created permit systems to monitor the numbers and species of animals being exported.

If a proposal is sound and there is a bona fide need for the requested animals, a permit is usually issued. Foreign officials who issue these permits are by no means fools. They usually recognize legitimate researchers as distinct from animal exploiters simply by scrutinizing each request for the species and number of animals requested.

Having the backing of a recognized scientific institution, such as a zoo, museum, or university, can certainly help when applying for a permit. In this respect, I have been extremely fortunate to have had such support from the Carnegie Museum of Natural History in Pittsburgh, Pennsylvania (my former place of employment and where I am still considered a field research associate). Consequently, specimens collected on my trips are preserved and deposited into the museum upon their deaths.

Standard protocols call for museum researchers to preserve, mount, prepare, and extract as much data from specimens as soon as possible after they are initially collected. This allows valuable information about reproduction, diet, and other such natural history observations to be retrieved and documented under specific circumstances. My research, however, is unique. Instead, I have tried to combine the workings of a museum person together with those of a zookeeper. By doing so, I have added a lot more work to my field research, but I feel justified in that each and every specimen is being utilized to its absolute maximum.

Even with all the preparations and research that went into planning my first trip to Costa Rica, I was nevertheless unprepared for the culture shock I was to experience. So much of what we take for granted here in the United States is a great luxury or an unreachable dream to the majority of third world countries. Even basics such as food, clothing, and shelter are often considered luxury items to a large number of people in these places.

I will never forget the terrible feeling of helplessness and depression I felt as I sat in a small restaurant in the coastal town of Limón in southeastern Costa Rica. While waiting for my food to be served, I noticed a small boy passing from table to table, trying to sell something to each of the patrons. Probably no more than eight years old, he was clad only in a pair of worn-out shorts. His small body, quite dirty, was noticeably muscular, indicating that he was no stranger to hard physical work. Around his neck he sported a torn and dingy cloth bag. He frequently reached into it to display his wares to the diners. With great patience, he humbly went through his rehearsed routine until almost everyone in the restaurant had been approached. A tourist couple sitting at a table close to mine were at first hesitant to make a purchase. The boy's gentle pleading and his pitiful appearance finally convinced the couple, and a few coins were finally exchanged for his merchandise. The woman carefully examined her purchase, then cautiously bit into the roundish, white object. Grimacing like a child swallowing a large spoonful of castor oil, she slowly drained the contents into her unwelcoming mouth. The gentleman, obviously seasoned in this routine, bit a small hole into the object and proceeded to empty its contents. With a nod of approval, he went on to finish a second and then a third one. With the last one in his outstretched hand, he offered it to the woman who was clearly hesitant to take it. She smiled weakly as she lowered her hand beneath the table then gave her wrist a quick flick sending the object close to my foot. My curiosity piqued, I bent down to examine the source of her discomfort. A cold shutter shot through my body as I stared at the collapsed mass in my hand. To my horror and disgust, I discovered that it was a sea turtle egg.

I was overcome by a range of emotions. As a herpetologist, I was livid that such actions could be perpetrated against such a magnificent creature, whose only crime was to come ashore each year to lay her eggs in the warm nurturing sand, as her species has done for millions of years. I was

saddened to think that the fate of one group of animals could be so nega-
tively influenced by the actions of another. Perhaps my greatest emotion
was fear. I was afraid there was little anyone could do to stop scenes like
this, which undoubtedly occur daily around the world. How could anyone convince this child that his daily egg raiding of this endangered species was so detrimental to the turtles' survival, without noticing that it
was also essential for his own survival?

•   •

To anyone planning a trip to Costa Rica, a visit to the Monteverde Cloud
Forest Reserve is a must. Located in the west-central region of the country, it represents the classic image of a pristine tract of virgin forest. Its
largely undisturbed biodiversity gives it its great appeal. Here a generalist
or specialist, a herpetologist or ornithologist, a novice or seasoned traveler can experience a profound bond with nature.

With improved maintenance over the years, the twenty-five miles of
largely gravel road have made the journey there much more bearable.
This, my first trip there, took more than three and a half hours, and I gave
serious thought to changing my citizenship rather than facing the long,
arduous drive back. Nonetheless, the jaunt was and is well worth the
trouble.

At the outskirts of the reserve are a few small villages where local people
live a simple and serene existence. They are mostly Quakers who emi-
grated from the United States during the late 1940s and have devoted their
lives to cultivation and development of dairy farms and seem unaffected
by the international interest that the reserve generates. Guests here may
visit their facilities, where they can watch cheese being made, after which
they can sample and purchase many homemade dairy products.

Capitalizing on the brisk tourist trade, several quaint hotels and *pensiones*
(a kind of boarding house) surround the reserve and allow for stays in a
more comfortable setting than camping out. For a modest fee, one can
rent a room with hot water and a meal and still be within walking distance of the reserve's wilderness.

One of the most famous wildlife residents of the Monteverde Reserve
is the golden toad *(Bufo periglenes)*. A three- to four-inch-long amphibian found nowhere else, it is one of the most strikingly beautiful of all
anurans. Males are a brilliant "Day-Glo" orange, in stark contrast to females, which are predominately brown with reddish-orange spots. The
toad's unusual natural history, coupled with its beauty and rarity, drew

Golden toads *(Bufo pereglenes)* in the Monteverde Cloud Forest, Costa Rica. Yellow and orange toads are males; the female is brown.

me to this wondrous place. Emergence and subsequent breeding of golden toads occur between April and June, although the toads are usually out and active for only about a two-week period. When small, temporary pools are created by excess moisture in the air and seasonal rains, brightly colored males congregate at these breeding sites and wait for females to arrive. When a female finally makes her way to a pool, several males may try to mate with her simultaneously, often creating a writhing knot of toads. To see one of these toads in the wild is a rare privilege; to witness their breeding behavior must rank as one of the greatest thrills in all of nature.

Although I was not lucky enough to get to the reserve at just the right time on this trip, I was fortunate enough to see several of these live toads firsthand. In a small building at the entrance to the reserve, where one must pay a nominal fee to visit the park, were several small terrariums—each containing examples of native herpetofauna. One of them contained two pairs of these exquisite amphibians. After I paid my fee and purchased about a dozen souvenir tee shirts, I asked the person in charge if I could photograph the toads outside their cage, preferably in a more naturalistic setting. To my surprise and delight, permission was granted, and within a few minutes I had exposed a full roll of film on these incredible toads.

I wondered why nature had created such a gaudy animal. The shockingly bright color of the male toad as it sat in my hand was more like some sort of battery-operated toy than a real living animal.

As I entered the Monteverde Cloud Forest, countless trees of varying sizes surrounded me, each adorned with numerous colorful bromeliads, orchids, creeping vines, and fungi. High in the treetops, I could hear the distinctive call of the spectacular three-wattled bellbird *(Procnias tricarunculata)*, a bird whose loud, gonglike voice is unlike any other in the Costa Rican rain forest. Living up to its name, the male possesses three distinctive, long whiskerlike projections that extend from around the base of its beak to nearly halfway down its chest. Although I never got a glimpse of this bird, its loud, strong, bell-like song was enough to make me feel tranquil and at peace in this marvelous paradise.

Scurrying around in the leaf litter were various species of frogs. Some blended in with their somber-colored surroundings while others were startlingly bright. Harlequin frogs *(Atelopus varius)* fearlessly ambled the forest floor, confident that their vivid coloration would warn off any possible predators. As I penetrated deeper into the forest, a thick mist refreshed me in its cool, lingering dampness. Mild temperatures kept most annoying insects away, but I was still bombarded by constant buzzing sounds. These sounds, however, were not produced by insects, but rather by wings of the nimble, aerial acrobats, hummingbirds. On any given day, more than a dozen species could be seen hovering around aromatic flowers on whose energy-rich nectar they fed.

I spent most of the day walking jungle trails that criss-crossed the reserve, hoping to catch a glimpse of every bird, bug, mammal, and herp in this seemingly endless expanse of greenery. Despite my patience and perseverance, I was able to sample only a small bit of this awe-inspiring forest.

Female harlequin frog *(Atelopus varius)* from the Monteverde Cloud Forest in Costa Rica. Females are the more attractive sex within this species.

Male harlequin frog
(Atelopus varius)
showing the more
somber coloration
of its sex.

This suited me fine, since it gave me an excuse to return again and again until I had seen it all. I can only hope that neither people nor nature will destroy this irreplaceable paradise and that I live to an old age so that I may continue to return and enjoy it.

••

Before leaving Texas, I had corresponded with several people in Costa Rica who shared my herpetological interests. One particular gentleman, an amateur herpetologist, invited me to accompany him on a day-long outing to collect poison frogs (*Dendrobates* sp.) for a research project. Because of his expertise of the local herpetofauna, I knew this would be an incredible opportunity for me to encounter some rare and outstanding herps.

We began by visiting one of his favorite spots in the central region of the country not far from the capital. As we walked near some small ponds heavily overgrown with aquatic and broadleaf plants, he suggested that I examine the underside of the leaves in the center of the pond. Naturally, those leaves were the most inaccessible (to me as well as to any predators). Sure enough, under a few of the leaves were several frail-looking, spindly legged treefrogs (*Hyla pseudopuma*). Continuing up and away from the water, we made our way into a small wooded area containing very little undergrowth, where a thick carpet of dead leaves blanketed the forest floor. In the woods we paused occasionally to listen for faint sounds of any rustling dead leaves that would give away a small animal's presence. Soon I became proficient with this technique, and in a matter of minutes I caught my first poison frog. I found that if I stared directly in front of me and walked exaggeratedly slowly, I could peripherally see any nearby movement, however slight. As a result, I could detect even the slightest movement of the smallest herp.

Seeing a poison frog in a book or on some televised nature show is interesting enough, but actually to view one in the wild is absolutely exhilarating. However, it is no easy task to catch one. They can be surprisingly agile, and when pursued in dense leaf litter, they are extremely elusive. Great care must be used when catching them, not so much because of their toxic skin secretions, but because one can sometimes forget how much force a diving herpetologist can exert on an inch-long animal.

Eight poison frog species in three different genera inhabit Costa Rica. I was pleased to have caught three species in one day. This was my first experience seeing these beautiful jewel-like frogs in the wild, and no matter how many of these exquisite amphibians I saw and photographed, my enthusiasm to search for more never waned. By day's end I must have seen several hundred poison frogs, although I kept only ten of each species, the limit of my research permit. With the capture of these frogs, in addition to any other reptile and amphibian kept during these expeditions, the workload increased exponentially. Part of our daily duties included the watering and feeding of any newly acquired animals. This means that at the beginning of each day, they had to be checked to ensure that they were well hydrated and had not been compromised due to temperature extremes. Fortunately, larger reptiles can go for extended periods of time (several weeks in many cases) without food. The smaller ones such as these poison frogs, however, needed to be fed every few days. Food items such as insects, arachnids, worms, etc., had to be caught daily. By the end of each trip, the time we spent caring for these new charges almost exceeded the time we spent in the field searching for new specimens.

While wandering through the woods, I encountered a small pile of cut logs, which I carefully disassembled until I reached the bottom layer. There I caught my first-ever caecilian. At first glance this glossy, legless amphibian looks like an earthworm with a glandular problem, but upon closer inspection one can see minute eyes and tiny "appendages" bordering its mouth. These appendages (actually "tentacles") are used to locate worms underground. To most wildlife collectors, this find might be dismissed as insignificant, yet catching an eighteen-inch-long Mexican caecilian (*Dermophis mexicanus*) was for me a significant accomplishment. Given the secretive and subterranean lifestyle of caecilians, as well as the fact that our knowledge concering their parasites is scant, this find provided a rare opportunity for me to delve into their biology—something which few biologists have undertaken. But this was still not *the* prize catch of the day. As we made our way back to our vehicle, my friend noticed something near a pile of sticks; it turned out to be an adult Picado's pit viper (*Atropoides [Bothrops] picadoi*), one of the rarest venomous snake species in Costa Rica. It remained there, coiled and completely oblivious to our presence, until we tried to capture it. When we disturbed it, the snake hissed loudly and struck at any nearby movement. Fortunately, after blocking its escape by placing a large collecting sack in front of it, we managed to secure it with little effort.

By the time we returned to our vehicle, word of our catch had spread to a number of the local residents. Before long, one of them approached us with a burlap sack in his hand, untied the bag, and poured its contents on the ground in front of us. To our surprise, he revealed yet another Picado's pit viper, slightly larger than the one we had caught earlier. Two specimens in one day—incredible. Unfortunately, the native was not as concerned with the snake's well-being, as we were. Halfway down the reptile's back was an open gash about four inches long through which its spine and internal viscera were visible. The man explained that he had caught the snake with his machete. Despite this severe injury, I was glad to obtain the snake, thinking that perhaps with care and medical treatment it would survive. Unfortunately, within a week of my return it died from its wounds. I preserved the specimen, which now is in the Carnegie Museum.

We returned to base camp, where we divided our catch. Since my friend's needs were limited, he gave me most of what we had collected. I asked him if he could accompany me to other parts of the country where we could find more choice spots, but with prior commitments to satisfy, he was unable to do so. He did, however, show me on a map some areas he thought would be to my liking. Armed with this information, I thanked him and bid him farewell.

• •

Driving west on Costa Rica Route 1, toward Guanacaste, I could hardly believe that I was still in the same country where earlier in the day I had found poison frogs and gaudy treefrogs in bromeliads in a cloud forest. Here, in the western province, the landscape is more like that of central and west Texas with its vast open savannas and its paucity of green vegetation. With its long dry season, Guanacaste Province is the center of Costa Rica's cattle industry, but it has not always been this way. Savannas resulted from activities of local farmers who cut and burned most of the forests, leaving only a few scattered trees in the resulting grasslands. Despite the lack of woodlands, this region is nonetheless rich in the diversity of its reptiles and amphibians.

I was advised to seek the help of a farmer who lived near the small village of Cañas. In addition to owning a sizable tract of land, the man also had a fair knowledge of the local herpetofauna. He was the kind of person who made friends easily, and anyone who met George took an instant liking to him. His unassuming nature and generous hospitality were among the reasons for my subsequent returns to his property. The most important, however, was the area's diversity of herps. On any given night, it was possible to cruise the roads and find as many as a dozen species of reptiles and amphibians, not including the mundane toads or nondescript lizards. On the second night, I saw what I first believed was a scorpion crossing the road. I stopped the car so that I could examine and perhaps photograph the creature, but to my surprise, it was not a scorpion at all, but a beautiful female elegant gecko (*Coleonyx mitratus*). This was a marvelous animal with broad black bands against velvety skin that seemed almost to phosphoresce. Just prior to my catching her, she stood on her toe tips and waved her tail in an attempt to look more ominous, and, as I gently grabbed her, she emitted a fairly audible squeak, protesting her capture.

I had planned my arrival to coincide with the onset of the rainy season in early June and to use this to my advantage to collect seldom-seen amphibians in this hot, dry region. As rains fell, temporary ponds formed, creating instant habitat for many frogs. One species I heard calling from these breeding sites one night was a rather large and robust toad (*Bufo leutkeni*). Males were bright lemon yellow, whereas females were various shades of light brown, with some dark spots. But the following morning, much to my surprise, the males, which had been bright yellow the night before, were now dark brown. Fortunately, I had photographed them while they were still calling the night before, thus documenting their color change. Among some other interesting species of frogs I found in this habitat were Mexican treefrogs (*Smilisca phaeota*), sheep frogs (*Hypopachus variolosus*), and the famous puddle frog, also known as the Túngara frog (*Physalaemus pustulosus*). Instead of laying its eggs in water as most frogs do, this species makes an unusual nest by rapidly whipping its hind legs together, then laying its eggs in the resulting protective foam. This foam nest helps keep the eggs moist should the temporary pool dry up before the offspring emerge. The way in which this frog copes with one of its main predators, the fringe-lipped bat *(Trachops cirrhosus)*, is interesting as well. Though all amphibians have poisonous skin secretions, some species are more toxic than others. The fringe-lipped bat has learned to recognize calls of more poisonous species and thus avoid them, thereby concentrating on the tastier ones. So, at night when male frogs call to attract mates, bats listen for this distinctive song, which often results in a frog's demise. To improve its survival potential, the puddle frog, which falls into the tasty category, has made some necessary adjustments to this scenario. At the first sign of a bat, a frog simply stops calling, takes a hop or two, and waits briefly until the danger has passed. When the threat is gone, it resumes its normal activities. Simple, but quite successful.

• •

With only a few days left before my scheduled return to the United States, I felt a sense of urgency to maximize my efforts to find last-chance treasures. There were still so many animals that I had not yet seen and so many that I promised myself I would make every effort to find.

Heading east through Cartago, I found the drive slightly more challenging than any I had experienced so far. The road took me through winding mountain passes with steep drop-offs and with no roadside guardrails. Adding to my anxiety were the numerous fast moving trucks that seemed reluctant to use their brakes. Obviously, the hazardous conditions made road collecting here impossible.

As I neared the village of Turrialba, about eighteen miles (thirty kilometers) from where I intended to spend the night, I saw a small, unusual snake crossing the road. I was pretty much out of the nightmarish mountainous-road-from-hell zone, so I felt that I could safely stop the car to catch it. As I bolted from the car, flashlight in hand, I was overcome by the panicky feeling researchers get when discovering that the "catch" of the trip has eluded them. Despite a frantic search, the snake was not to be found. Dejected and angry at myself, I returned to the car and turned on the bright lights to illuminate as much of the road as possible. Now I was able to see a faint movement at the edge of the pavement. Had I waited another five seconds, the snake would have disappeared into the thick grass along the roadside. Standing above the snake, I realized why I had had such a difficult time finding it. It was tiny, only about eight inches long, and its coloration perfectly matched that of the road. The only tell-tale sign that made it visible was its white head. I had never seen a snake like this before, and I could not hazard a guess what it was. At first, I thought it was some kind of mutant coral snake that lacked red pigment. Closer examination ruled out that possibility. There are only four species of coral snakes in Costa Rica, and this snake was too small and dissimilar in coloration to be confused with any of them.

When I finished fantasizing about new species and range extensions, I did the only other thing I could think of—that is, search for additional specimens. As luck would have it, I was able to find one more of these bizarrely colored snakes. It was not until I returned to the States that I was finally able to properly identify them. They were *Enuliophis* [*Enulius*] *sclateri*, a small, elusive snake that lives much of its life under leaf litter or in rotten logs.

Two o'clock in the morning, and the adrenalin rush of finding some unusual animals had rapidly faded. I was beginning to nod at the wheel. I pulled over to the side of the road and closed my eyes for a few minutes in the hope of recharging myself. I shut off the engine, took a long swig from a bottle of warm orange soda, and settled down in the front seat. As I did, I heard a loud anuran call coming from the ditch next to the car, followed by several more. I soon realized that I would get no rest here.

Flashlight in hand, I slowly made my way to the nearby weeds. Naturally, when you shine a light on or near a calling amphibian, you are sure to get total silence. A few seconds later, the chorus started up again, and I was finally able to get a glimpse of what was making all that racket. From the center of the weeds, I counted several thin and spindly Lancaster's treefrogs *(Hyla lancasteri)*. Once I knew where to look, pinpointing their hiding places was easy. One call, however, sounded quite different from the others. It took me a while longer, but eventually my patience was rewarded when I found a bizarre-looking frog, *Rana warschewitschii*. With its pointed and elongated head, it resembled no other frog familiar to me. This was a great place to herp, but I desperately needed sleep. I decided to drive the remaining few miles to the town of Siquirres.

I was never good at sleeping while sitting upright in a car. Add to that the fact that mosquitoes make wonderful natural alarm clocks, and you begin to see why it is impossible to get too much sleep slumped over a steering wheel in a tropical country. After a refreshing 140 minutes of tossing, turning, sweating, and continual bug slapping, I had to face a new day.

Trying to get my bearings, I noticed I had chosen an excellent place to stop for the night. Apparently, I was on the outskirts of town, parked next to a small stream adjacent to a wooded lot. Spilling out of the car and trying to get some blood back into my legs, I hobbled along the stream as I looked for signs of life. By the time I could walk upright again, I saw movement next to rocks at the water's edge. The brilliant red coloration of the dainty-looking strawberry poison frog was visible at quite a distance. Even in such open areas, this amphibian has little to fear from predators, for its bright coloration gives fair warning of its potent toxins. Climbing the modest bank along the water, I found myself in a wooded area where few of the sun's rays penetrated to the forest floor. In this shaded and dimly lit spot, I found several exquisite phallus-laced mushrooms (*Dictyophora indusiata*), a species with a white, fairly large (apple-sized) mushroom whose cap is an intricate network of delicate-looking lace. I had seen pictures of these fungi before, but never a living specimen. A closer look revealed numerous small black flies swarming around the top of the fungus. As I stood there, staring at the mushrooms, I was treated to a spectacular sight. A poison frog hopped from under nearby leaf litter, took up a position beneath the large mushroom cap, and almost immediately began to feed on the flies by using its remarkably fast and adhesive tongue. Moments later, several more poison frogs gathered under the same mushroom to partake of the feast. Soon, about ten poison frogs from two different species had gathered, making for a most spectacular sight.

• •

Near the end of my trip, hours seemed to tick away like seconds. Before I knew it, I had to pack up my equipment and head home. I still had so much to do, foremost of which was the matter of obtaining export permits for the specimens in my possession, and I thought it best to keep the rented vehicle as long as possible. Finally, with only about twenty-four hours remaining before my departure, I was free to try to enjoy the last precious moments in the capital. Before unloading the car, I had a snack at a little pizza place across the street from my hotel. Eagerly wolfing down my food, as I am known to do, I was out of the restaurant in less than fifteen minutes. As I returned to the car, which was only fifty feet from the café and directly across the street from my hotel on a busy thoroughfare, I noticed that the driver's door was unlocked. I thought this strange; I was positive I had locked it. As I walked to the back of the car, I noticed that the back door was also unlocked. I was now beginning to feel ill. A chill ran through me and my heart was pounding like a jackhammer. As I opened the back door, my worst fears were confirmed: the car had been burglarized. Nearly everything in the vehicle was gone. My camera bag and its contents, my clothing, gifts I had purchased for practically everyone in the United States—everything. I could not move or speak or even catch my breath. As the shock wore off, I noticed one item was left untouched in the back of the car. It was the huge box that contained all the specimens, the only thing that was truly irreplaceable. Yet this was no time for celebration. The break-in could not have happened more than a few minutes earlier, and I was sure that the thieves might still be nearby.

I ran into the lobby of my hotel and quickly explained to the desk clerk what had happened. He showed no sympathy; instead he chastised me for leaving my things unattended in a car—just what I wanted to hear at that moment. I ran back to the car, retrieved the box of animals, and locked them in my hotel room. I hoped the thieves might have discarded some of my things as they ran from my car. More than anything, I prayed I might recover some of the spent film, but it just was not meant to be. When I think back on all those once-in-a-lifetime photos I probably will never get again, I still want to scream. Despite my frantic search in every nearby yard, bush, and corner, there was no trace of any of my belongings. I went to the nearest police station to file a report. Here again, there was no sympathy. I was assured that if I provided all the serial numbers from my camera equipment, they would do everything in their power to recover the stolen items. Fortunately, I did have a list of all the serial numbers. Unfortunately, that list was safely tucked away in the side compartment of my stolen camera bag. I had to call my friend in the States who was house-sitting for me and have her read me the numbers from the list that I had left behind.

While Debbie was thrilled to hear from me, she certainly was not pleased to learn what happened. Although there was little she could do, her reassurance and positive attitude did much to lift my badly broken spirits. Somehow, after talking with her, everything seemed better. I returned to the police station with the list of serial numbers and left with a copy of the police report, which I assumed I would need to show my friends, who might accuse me of being so cheap that I bought them nothing.

There was still one more task: to clean and return the car to the rental agency. With the stench of old smelly socks, formalin-soaked paper towels, and pieces of half-eaten food strewn about the seats, a distinctively foul odor permeated the car. I began operation "forklift" from the rear of the car and worked my way to the front. Although I had already amassed a rather large bag of trash, I still had not touched the piles at the front of the car. As I cleaned out the glove compartment, I experienced perhaps the greatest feeling of elation of the entire trip. There, amidst the car's papers and the badly folded maps, under the candy wrappers and the spent batteries, I found a single roll of exposed film. The sight of that roll of film in my hand was like getting a last-minute reprieve from the governor. I was so thrilled with my good fortune that I looked skyward and shouted, "Yes, yes, thank you—*thank you*." Of course I had no idea what images were on that roll, but that actually made it even better. Now I had something special to look forward to. Was it the roll with the crocodile basking on the shore in Guanacaste? Perhaps it was the scene of the poison frogs feeding on the flies in Siquirres, or maybe even something from Monteverde? I felt so good that I was no longer bothered by what had happened just a few hours earlier.

After cleaning out the car, I had a huge bag of trash to throw away. Unlike in the United States, which has numerous garbage cans or large dumpsters on nearly every street corner, I was unable to find a suitable place to discard my rubbish. I thought for a moment, then jokingly decided to lock the trash in the car and let the thieves come back to steal my garbage. In the time it took to walk back to my hotel room, splash some water on my face, and return to the car, the deed was done. Sure enough, someone had broken into the car and made off with my trash.

On my return to Houston I felt like a conquering hero. Enthusiastic friends surrounded me. They envied my triumphs and sympathized with my tribulations. I repeated my stories again and again, and of course with each retelling, some small amount of embellishment was added. However, the truth be known, Costa Rica is a land of spectacular beauty and wonder, and that is no exaggeration.

• •

After the "umpteenth" time of retelling the story of how I was burglarized, someone asked me matter-of-factly if my insurance company had covered my losses. I had a blank stare on my face, thought for a minute, then blurted out, "Yeah, right, are you serious?" How could I possibly be compensated for such a loss, and particularly in a foreign country? When I called my insurance company and told the agent what had happened, he asked me for a copy of the police report. I informed him that I had one, but it was in Spanish. He said to send it along with copies of as many receipts of the stolen items as I could find. He also asked me to determine the total value of all the stolen items. I gave him a rough estimate and was told to wait for a response.

I spent the next several days searching for five-, six-, and even seven-year-old receipts that related to the stolen equipment. This itself was a monumental task. A few days later, before I even had a chance to send in my paperwork, I received a letter from my insurance company. Unbelievably, it contained a check covering the loss of all my belongings. Even to this day, many years later, I still have not sent the requested paperwork, and I have not heard another word from the company regarding this incident.

By the way, the roll of film that I found in the glove compartment was a roll I had shot in the Monteverde Cloud Forest and it was almost entirely of the beautiful golden toads, a species now believed extinct and which can never be photographed again.

CHAPTER 2

A Return to Paradise, More Endless Roads

IT WAS MAY, 1984, less than a year since my last trip, and I was anxious to return to Costa Rica. Having previously spent only three weeks there, I had barely scratched the surface of that wondrous paradise. All I had to show for my earlier efforts was a single roll of exposed film; you can imagine how difficult it is to impress an audience with a three-minute slide show.

When I announced my intention to return to Costa Rica, I had no shortage of friends willing to help "carry my bags." Since I was still a novice traveler, I was not comfortable with the idea of a group of people crammed into a car with me, gobbling up containers of Nō-Dōz tablets and sharing gallons of eyedrops as we spent every waking moment with our eyes glued to the road. I finally relented and invited just one friend to join me, but after a few days in the field with me, I did not know if she would ever be the same.

Vickie is a talented artist who hoped to capture on canvas some of Costa Rica's remarkable natural treasures. For my part, I expected to see every species of reptile and amphibian I had failed to observe on my first trip.

It is a common mistake to believe that after doing something only once, you qualify as an expert. So, it is quite sobering when you think you know it all, only to be knocked down a peg or two by your own overconfidence. This was vividly demonstrated on one of the first nights of road collecting. We found herps everywhere and preserved any reptile or amphibian found dead on the road in formalin (a dilute solution of formaldehyde) so that it could be deposited later in a museum collection. I was euphoric, and I could not help showing off to Vickie.

"That's *Bufo coccifer*. This small snake is *Geophis hoffmanni*," I spouted in Latin. Though most of these animals have no common names, I suppose I could have toned it down a bit by saying: "This is a type of toad" or "this is a species of skink." One of the snakes I saw on the road had been recently hit by a vehicle but was still intact and in good overall condition. I studied the twenty-inch-long reptile for a moment but could not make a positive identification. Since it was so boldly marked and distinctively colored, the snake should have been easily recognizable. Vickie watched as I stuttered and stammered in a vain attempt to explain why I could not rattle off its scientific name. Here was a great opportunity for her to put me in my place for being a "know-it-all," but instead she let me off the hook by saying, "No big deal, it's obviously a rare and obscure snake."

If only that were the case; after all, how obscure can a bright red snake with a black head be? (More on that later.)

• •

As it had been the previous year, one of my priorities on this trip was to visit the cloud forest of Monteverde. Since I again timed my arrival to coincide with the emergence of golden toads, I was hoping to be in the right place at the right time. Before beginning the daylong walk through the reserve, we stopped at the park entrance and paid the modest visiting fee. Once again, I performed the traditional, buy-every-tee-shirt-they-had routine, followed by the traditional can-I-please-take-a-picture-of-your-golden-toads routine. This time, however, the visitors' center had only a single male toad in one of their cages; the rest were empty. When I asked about the possibility of seeing this species in the wild, I received the reply that I had come too early for that. "Perhaps in a few weeks" was the response. This was very disappointing, since one of my main objectives was at least to glimpse these rare toads in their natural environment.

Lack of toads notwithstanding, there was still much to see. As we walked through the reserve, we could hear the gonglike calls of the three-wattled bellbird, a bird that had captivated me almost a year ago by its distinctive, metallic song—"Boinggg-boinggg." This bird is a member of the cotinga family, whose varied species include the two rare cock-of-the-rocks (*Rupicola* sp.) and the even more bizarre-looking umbrella bird (*Cephalopterus sp.*), so named because of its large, preposterous head crest, especially evident in males.

Trampling through the brush in hopes of encountering wildlife is often a losing proposition. Small animals such as frogs, lizards, and especially birds are attuned to the slightest movements and disturbances and will flee or quickly conceal themselves when approached. I find that the best way to observe forest creatures is to move slowly and quietly, pause frequently, then stand perfectly still. At first the untrained eye sees little, but with patience, rewards can be great. This applies not only in MonteVerde, but wherever wildlife is found.

The farther I penetrated into the woods, the more interesting and exotic the wildlife became. In addition to the occasional frog scampering amidst the thick layer of ground cover, several other interesting amphibians were evident. Similar in appearance and behavior to some of the poison frogs is the beautifully colored, little anuran known as the harlequin frog *(Atelopus varius).* Unlike most animal species of which males are considered the more attractive sex, in this species the female is the uncontested beauty. Males are smaller than females, with a light green coloration that pales in comparison to the vivid black-and-yellow dorsum of females. Some females even have splashes of fire red coloration on their backs and bellies. In fact, this species varies so greatly in coloration that more than a dozen distinctive color varieties are known. I collected several specimens and spent nearly an hour photographing and then releasing them. Although I had a permit to collect many local amphibians and reptiles, I was not allowed to remove *any* animals from the nature reserve, particularly this protected species.

Equally handsome, and perhaps even gaudier than the harlequin frog, is the spectacular red-eyed treefrog *(Agalychnis callidryas).* Without doubt, this is the "peacock" of amphibians. As its name suggests, this frog's eyes are blood red, but the vivid color is visible only when its eyes are fully open. A semitransparent membrane covering its large eyes veils the color when the amphibian is snoozing or in a restful state. Being nocturnal, the frog spends daylight hours clinging to the underside of leaves, where its green coloration helps it blend in with its surroundings. While asleep, the frog remains motionless with its eyes tightly closed and almost sunken into its head. It resembles part of the leaf. Watching the frog's eyes opening is a phenomenal sight. Upon awakening, the anuran's semitransparent membranes recede from its eyes as they rise up from its head like headlights on a foreign sports car. When the frog changes its posture, it reveals

Red-eyed treefrog
(*Agalychnis
callidryas*) from
the rain forests
of Costa Rica.

a body covered with a rainbow of colors. Its feet and toes are yellowish orange, and as it begins its slow and deliberate walk across the surface of the leaf, the frog reveals patches of brilliant blue and purple on its sides. After witnessing the beauty of a red-eyed treefrog, I am tempted to call it a day, since anything else I might find later would seem mundane by comparison.

Another cloud forest frog I very much wanted to find, although I was not completely certain it was a frog at all, was heard calling all day. While I had heard the distinct sound nearly everywhere in Costa Rica, I was never able to trace it to its source. Until now, I had assumed the vocalization came from a frog, although I realized it could have been made easily by an insect or perhaps even a bird. I decided I would now search for this invisible caller that so far had eluded me. Hearing the call was easy, but pinpointing its exact location was another matter. Vickie and I converged over a small bush where we were certain the animal was located. As soon as we got close, the call ceased; after a brief pause, it began again. Each time we heard the sound, Vickie and I simultaneously pointed to where we thought it originated, but our fingers were never in agreement. After nearly thirty minutes of this frustrating ventriloquist's game, we were totally exasperated. This was absurd. Even though we were hunched over a bush no more than four feet tall, we were unable to locate this pleasant but taunting call. Finally, when our patience ran thin, Vickie started a leaf-by-leaf search, beginning at the base of the bush. Seconds later she exclaimed, "I found him." There in the axil of the foliage was a tiny, three-quarter-inch-long, brown, drab-looking frog. I found it hard to believe that so small an animal could make such a big noise. We later learned that it is known by several names, including "tink" frog or "dink" frog, in reference to its call, which sounds like two Coke bottles being hit together. Its scientific name, *Eleutherodactylus diastema,* is many times longer than the frog itself. I regretted not having a tape recorder to capture its call.

By late afternoon, we made it back to the car. To prolong our departure, I tried every delaying tactic I could think of, but with darkness approaching, we had to face reality. As we began the arduous drive down the mountain, I felt compelled to make one more foray into the nearby woods. Pulling over, I parked near several large, rotten logs. This seemed ideal amphibian habitat, and after flipping over pieces of the decaying woodpile, I was rewarded by finding a pair of palm salamanders *(Bolitoglossa robusta)*. Like most salamanders, they were not very colorful. These were solid black with a faint orange band around the base of their tails. As the name *robusta* implies, this species is larger than most other palm salamanders—nearly seven inches long.

• •

Because my last trip to Costa Rica had been so successful, I had high hopes for a repeat performance. By journey's end, I would not be disappointed. Although I did not find large numbers of reptiles and amphibians, I did find an enormous diversity of species crossing the roads. Timing in these matters is crucial; were it not for the onset of the rainy season, my success would have been more modest.

Driving down the main highway, I was both elated and disappointed to find a rainbow boa *(Epicrates cenchria)*: elated because this was a young snake with a bold, vibrant color pattern—not a very common species—and disappointed because it had recently been hit by a car and was dead on the road. At least I was able to preserve the snake for a museum collection, thus preventing it from being wasted and becoming ant fodder.

Not long thereafter, I was pleased to see a long, slender snake crawling across the road. Its large, bulbous head and astonishingly thin neck left little doubt that this was a blunt-headed tree snake *(Imantodes gemmistratus)*, another classic serpent of tropical America. It reaches a length of about four feet, with a body barely thicker than a pencil, an adaptation for living in trees and bushes, where it feeds primarily on small arboreal lizards and frogs. It subdues its prey with a mild venom, but its bite poses no threat to humans. Its weak toxins quickly immobilize its prey, thereby reducing potential injury to the snake. Gentle and inoffensive, blunt-headed tree snakes are sometimes kept by reptile enthusiasts as pets.

As we drove farther west, we noticed a dramatic change in both the habitat and its wildlife. Instead of the mostly arboreal species we had encountered earlier, many of the animals we now saw on the road were terrestrial. Light rains brought out numerous frogs and toads, many of which could be seen in roadside shallow pools. Searching such miniature ponds sometimes revealed cat-eyed snakes *(Leptodeira annulata)* on the prowl for their dinner of small amphibians. Also in search of food during the welcome rains was the showy, tricolored slug-eating snake *(Sibon anthracops)*. These orange-, black-, and white-banded snakes feed almost entirely on slugs and snails. Possessing a modified lower jaw helps them to extract snails from their shells; they are well equipped to prey on these soft-bodied invertebrates. Of the seven species of slug-eaters in Costa Rica, this is the most attractive.

We arrived in Cañas at 9:00 P.M. My plan was to return to La Pacifica, my friend George's hotel, where we would rent rooms for the duration of our stay in northwestern Costa Rica. I calculated we would remain there about four days before we headed back to the country's eastern zone.

• •

After checking into our extremely modest rooms (essentially a bed and a door), we were invited over to George's home for dinner. It was good to see George again, and he was pleased to welcome me back to his residence, as were his wife, Lydia, and their three children. After some small talk and presentation of a few token gifts of candy for the kids, we sat

Tricolored slug-eating snake *(Sibon anthracops)* found crossing the road in northwestern Costa Rica.

down to a delicious home-cooked meal. George had spread the word to the local farmers to watch for specimens. He told us that many snakes had been turning up on his property, brought out primarily by the recent daily rains.

Since it was late, I thanked our hosts for their generous hospitality and excused myself so that I could retire for the night in anticipation of an early morning start to collect herps. I found it difficult to sleep, not because of the excessive heat or someone playing loud music, but because I could not put out of my mind the idea of the area's abundant wildlife. As I entered the communal bathroom to wash up, I got a glimpse of a gecko as it darted quickly behind the mirror. I dropped my toothbrush and soap, and my reward was a leaf-toed gecko (*Phyllodactylus tuberculosus*). This naturally led me to remove every mirror and wall hanging in the vicinity. Before I dozed off, I had collected three of the six gecko species known to occur in the northwestern province.

The next morning, I awoke early, anxious to get started. Since she had been up late the night before, Vickie chose to stay at the hotel to lounge around the pool and work on her art. Armed with pillowcases, plastic bags, a snake hook, and large rubber bands, I made my way to the sanctity of the nearby woods.

What made this forest so appealing was that it bordered the large Corobicí River, which, according to George, is a haven for countless species of reptiles. Here I had spotted a basking, six-foot-long crocodile last year. As I wandered through the woods, I could hear rustling sounds of lizards as they foraged through dense leaf litter. Sometimes I glimpsed an ameiva (a foot-long species related to the tegu lizards of South America) sunning itself in a patch of sunlight on the otherwise dimly lit forest floor. If I was patient and remained still, I could see an anole or skink at my feet, rooting around the leaves in search of insects. But whenever I raised my hand to catch one, I failed, as it dived for cover and disappeared from view. The only way I consistently captured these elusive lizards was with an oversized rubber band. By placing the rubber band on the end of my forefinger and stretching it back for maximum power, I could hit small, fast-moving targets as far away as ten to fifteen feet. To prevent serious injury or even death to small and fragile species, the collector needs to become proficient by continually practicing this "art." Yet too soft a blow can result in an escaped lizard.

I had been at this for over an hour, and I must admit that the lizards were far ahead on points. After catching a few of only the more common species, I was ready to turn back to find a more productive area. At precisely 9:24 in the morning, my luck changed. Coming toward me was an absolutely gorgeous three-foot-long milk snake *(Lampropeltis triangulum stuarti)*. I was concerned that if I moved too soon or lunged at it before it cleared the thick tangle of underbrush, the snake would escape and I would never forgive myself. When the snake was one body length away from me, I held my breath, dove, and grabbed it just above its tail. The snake immediately turned, seized my hand, and bit viciously. I could not have cared less. I had a rare prize in my hands or, more correctly, it had me. I bagged the snake, washed the blood from my hands, and headed back to the hotel, grinning from ear to ear.

By late morning, with the temperature at nearly ninety degrees, collecting became almost impossible; only the hardiest animals can brave such extremes and, even then, just for brief periods (myself included). Among the lizards that can endure high temperatures are the ameivas and spiny-tailed iguanas *(Ctenosaura similis)*, both common species not worth risking heat stroke to chase. I usually take advantage of this "lull" time to photograph the day's catch or work on my field notes.

The days are relatively short in this part of the world, and by 6:00 P.M. it was almost dark. For some reason, I felt that tonight had great potential, but then again, every night has great potential in a country like Costa Rica.

The evening started slowly. Although the usual amphibians were active, they were present neither in large numbers nor in a great variety of species. As any steadfast herper will verify, when there are no animals on the road, a person finds it extremely difficult to keep from nodding at the wheel. This was the case tonight; that is, until 11:45 P.M., when my "wake-up" call came. I was on the last road trip of the night, having just passed through the town of Liberia, when my headlights picked up the reflection of a slender, twelve-inch-long object on the blacktop.

Reptile collectors who spend a lot of time road collecting do not need to see a real snake on the pavement to get the same charge as a shot of adrenalin. Merely seeing ordinary objects such as sticks, pieces of tires, and especially the dreaded fan-belt "snake" can instantly shock collectors back to consciousness. This time it was no mirage. I bolted out of the car just as the snake reached the edge of the pavement. In the beam of my flashlight I gave it a good long stare before grabbing it. (I have heard stories about collectors who, rather than lose a snake, will grab even a venomous one and quickly fling it back onto the road to prevent its escape. Though I consider myself a "hardcore" collector, I would never take such a foolish chance and risk a venomous snakebite, especially in a foreign country.) This was a juvenile Mexican burrowing python *(Loxocemus bicolor)*. Its common name is somewhat misleading, as no true pythons occur in the New World. Years ago, this species was classified as a member of the boa and python family. Further studies showed that it is not closely related to these constrictors, so it was later placed in its own family: Loxocemidae. This is a fascinating snake that spends much of its time underground or hidden deep in layers of dead leaves. It is a beautiful serpent with an iridescent bluish gray sheen over its entire body. Little is known about its natural history, although a recent article described a specimen that was found with its stomach full of sea turtle eggs. It is rarely kept in captivity, and despite concerted efforts, all attempts to breed it have up until this point been unsuccessful.

• •

The following morning I met with George and showed him the fruits of my labor. He was not surprised to see the milk snake; he said they appear on his property with some regularity. But the burrowing python had him nodding in approval.

"That's a nice find," he said, "but if you want more, I can take you to another place where they are more common." Needless to say, he did not have to ask twice.

Returning to the hotel, I asked Vickie to help me load the jeep with our collecting paraphernalia, then drove back to George's to pick up his family. With his wife and three children secured safely in the back of the vehicle, the seven of us were on our way. We headed west and were just past the point where I had found the burrowing python the night before when George instructed me to slow down and turn left at the next road, about a hundred meters ahead. As I approached my turn, a vehicle to my right suddenly, and without signaling, cut in front of me to make the same left turn. I was already completing the turn, however, and as any student of physics knows, two objects cannot occupy the same space at the same time. The result: one vehicle bent up like a pretzel, the other, broadsided and knocked over into a ditch. Inside our vehicle there was crying, screaming, and just plain pandemonium, but fortunately there were no serious injuries. I quickly ran to the ditch, anxious to see if the other driver was all right. His pickup truck was on its side at the bottom of the culvert. The windshield, through which he had been thrown, had turned into thousands of little glass pellets that were strewn everywhere. The driver, who had been ejected from the car, was staggering aimlessly about, holding his bloodied head, and muttering to himself in Spanish. After determining that his family was all right, George raced over to the other driver and demanded to know why he had acted so irresponsibly.

However, the other driver was in no condition to offer an explanation. Besides, George said he smelled alcohol on the driver's breath and was sure he had been drinking. By now the local police had arrived and asked for an account of what had happened. George basically told them that the other driver was at fault and that I did the best I could to prevent a more serious accident. The police ordered both drivers to report to a nearby hospital for a blood test. Apparently, this is standard procedure for anyone involved in an automobile accident.

Our car was in bad shape, although still driveable; the other vehicle was totaled and was being towed away. Its driver now had to find his own way to the hospital.

Let me say at this point that I *do not* like hospitals. I had never been sick a day in my life, I had never broken a bone in my body, and I still have my tonsils and appendix. With great care, I had thus far avoided these maladies, but now I was being forced to forfeit my spotless health record and submit to a hospital visit because some fool felt it necessary to practice his James Bond driving techniques in front of me.

The hospital in Liberia, as expected, was very modest and extremely overcrowded. People were lined up outside the front door, lying down in the halls, and in general occupying every square inch of available space. I chose to sit outside in the shade where the sounds and smells of my surroundings were only slightly diminished by the meager distance I tried to put between the building and myself.

Several hours passed before I was finally summoned to an examination room. Here I was to have a blood sample taken to determine if I was intoxicated when the accident took place (over three hours earlier). A nurse approached me and asked if I was feeling all right. George, who acted as my translator, explained to the nurse that I was involved in a car accident and that I was here to have a blood sample drawn to determine my state of sobriety. The nurse instructed me to extend my right arm and make a fist, then tied a piece of string around my bicep and attempted to insert a needle into one of my veins. I kept my head turned so I would not have to watch the syringe fill with blood. After feeling the needle pierce my arm for the third, then fourth time, I threw caution to the wind and finally faced my tormentor. In a loud and irritated voice I shrieked, "What the hell are you doing to me?" George's rather meek translation of "Que paso?" returned the explanation that she was unable to find a suitable vein. Eventually she made the appropriate adjustments, and voilà, a single drop of blood found its way into the 10 cc syringe. After additional manipulations, she managed to collect approximately one-third of the required amount. Apparently something was wrong with the syringe that was preventing blood from flowing into it freely. Looking back now, I shudder to think how many times the same needles and syringes may have been used and on how many people. Fortunately, AIDS was not a major consideration at the time, but there was still a chance of contracting some other debilitating disease. The nurse removed the syringe while the needle was still in my arm and replaced it with a "new" one. As she reached for the replacement, she let several drops trickle out from the needle, and it fell to the floor. When she was alerted to this, she merely placed a test tube beneath the steady drip of blood to collect the rest of the sample.

The entire incident obviously put a damper on the rest of the trip. Instead of spending the precious remaining time herping, I now had to deal with an extremely upset car rental agency. And if that was not bad enough, a lawyer representing the driver who had caused the accident later contacted me. He informed me that unless I paid for the complete repair of his car (of course it was a family heirloom, worth many thousands of dollars), I would not be allowed to leave the country. Although I really did not consider the action that much of a threat, I was nonetheless obliged to defend myself. The solution, according to George, was to hire my own attorney and have him take care of everything. This whole concept did not sit well with me from the beginning, but I knew I was in a no-win situation. My biggest disadvantage was that I was an American, and therefore, the locals assumed I must be rich. Although I am anything but rich, compared to most local people, I was wealthy. It was an uphill battle to convince my attorney and the driver of the other car that I was not made of money. When it was all over, I had given my last dollar to the lawyer, but now I was again a free man: free to return to the capital and wallow in self-pity. Once again, I was unable to purchase even a single souvenir for my friends back home. (They will never believe me.)

• •

With just two days left before our scheduled return, I had only one remaining task, the one I dreaded most on every research trip: the final visit to the permit office. This was always the "moment of truth," whether or not I would be issued a permit to export all the animals I had collected. This time, instead of just submitting a list of specimens for export, I turned in a large number of preserved animals, along with the pertinent locality data for each. By doing this, I was trying to show the authorities that I was not thinking of just myself; I was also contributing to their local herpeto- logical facility.

Basically, the permit system works like this: once the fieldwork is done, I submit a list of specimens for export. The permit authorities look it over to assure that none of the animals is protected and that I have not asked for some outrageous quantity of rare or threatened species. A per- mit is then issued, listing the species approved for export. But first, I must present the permit office with a list of everything I have collected, includ- ing preserved material.

Remember the bright red snake I collected on one of my first nights out? Well, I still had no clue what it might be. Although I did not know what it was, I was relatively certain of what it was not. By a process of elimination, I removed from consideration the species I thought it could not be. This may sound confusing, but it gets better. In spite of my di- lemma, I eventually had to choose a name for the permit office. After much deliberation, I narrowed my choice to ten possible species. I then threw an imaginary dart, only to have it land next to the name: *Trimetopon viquezi*. Fortunately, the permit office approved my request for all the specimens, including the aforementioned "*Trimetopon*."

When I returned to the United States, I believed that the matter of permits was now over, but several weeks later, I received a letter from Dr. Douglas C. Robinson, curator of herpetology at the University of Costa Rica, who had been sent a copy of the list of herpetological specimens I had recently exported. Apparently, my list had created quite a stir at the university due to one of the animals I collected. According to Dr. Robinson, the very rare snake *Trimetopon viquezi* is known only from a single speci- men; that snake, which was preserved many years ago, was deposited in a museum but has since been lost. In a sense, he was saying that I had the only known specimen in existence. He urged me to contact him as soon as possible to confirm this incredible herpetological breakthrough. Since I had been back only a short time, I had not yet sent any of the preserved specimens to the Carnegie Museum. (The museum eventually identifies all of my specimens, alerting me to any discrepancies.) The urgency of Dr. Robinson's letter, however, dictated that I act promptly to identify the questionable snake.

I immediately telephoned the Carnegie and told my former boss, Dr. Jack McCoy, what had occurred. He asked to see the snake as soon as possible, after which he would telephone me and reveal its correct identification. After several days of nail biting and handwringing, I finally heard from Dr. McCoy. The conversation went like this:

"Hello, Paul, this is Jack. You're kidding, right?" (Not exactly the start of a phone call that is supposed to announce with great fanfare the rediscovery of a snake once considered extinct.)

"Kidding, what do you mean?" I asked as my voice trailed off in a nervous laugh.

"Paul, where is this rare snake you supposedly sent; was it eaten on the way by this juvenile *Clelia clelia*?"

"A what?" I shrieked. "No way that's a *Clelia*," I said. "I know what they look like, and that's not even close."

"Paul, have you ever seen a juvenile of the species?" There was no reply. I was too embarrassed to speak. Here I was, Mr. World Traveler, Mr. Know-It-All, now humbled by the juvenile coloration of a common snake.

"Are you sure?" I asked meekly. Jack's hearty laugh answered my question.

Great. Not only had I humiliated myself in front of the one person I wanted to impress the most, but now I had to do it again (this time internationally) by writing to Dr. Robinson and explaining that I could not tell the difference between one of the rarest and one of the most common snake species in Costa Rica.

I wrote Dr. Robinson and explained the sequence of events from the time I found the snake to my phone call to the Carnegie. I apologized for

Juvenile mussurana (*Clelia clelia*) found dead on the road in Costa Rica. Note the bright red coloration and black head pattern typical of juveniles of this species.

the misunderstanding, blaming it on my lack of field experience. I never thought I would hear from him again, assuming he would write me off as some sort of lunatic. I did receive a follow-up letter from him, though, and the communication was sympathetic and understanding. He also expressed to me that it was refreshing to have a bona fide researcher apply for permits instead of having to deal with the typical wildlife dealer who is interested only in exploiting the country's flora and fauna.

• •

The snake that caused all the commotion, *Clelia clelia,* is known by the common name of mussurana. A member of the colubrid family, it can reach a length of over eight feet. It is also rear-fanged, which means that it possesses enlarged teeth in the back of its mouth from which mild venom flows along grooves then slowly makes its way into the victim. It feeds almost exclusively on snakes, most notably the terciopelo, a.k.a. the Central American lancehead *(Bothrops asper),* and, like kingsnakes of North America, it is nearly immune to bites of its venomous prey. Also of note (and something I will never forget) is that with age this species goes through a color change: from bright red in juveniles, with a black head, to a uniform bluish black in adults. Although it is unlikely that I will make the same mistake again with respect to the mussurana, I am still not out of the woods. This is especially true when one considers that many snake species (as well as frogs and lizards) go through some kind of pattern or color change at some point in their lives.

CHAPTER 3

Beefworms in Belize

I HAD BEEN HOME less than a week when I received a call from my mentor, Dr. Jack McCoy, at the Carnegie Museum. He called to ask if I wanted to participate in a herpetological research project in Belize, Central America. Since I still had not unpacked from my recent Costa Rica trip, I told him to count me in; I would meet him at the airport in fifteen minutes. He laughingly informed me that the trip was not scheduled for another three weeks. I could not believe my good fortune. Not only was I being asked to accompany the Carnegie on such a prestigious outing, but the museum was also going to pick up all my expenses. Was it the specimens I had donated in the past that prompted the invitation or my dedication to long, arduous fieldwork under harsh conditions? Or maybe it was my incessant daily phone calls begging to be invited on any future trip that the museum planned. Whatever it was, I really did not care; I was in.

The project was ambitious; a complete herpetological survey of the country, the results of which would hopefully lead to a photographic field guide (ideally using my photos). This effort would, no doubt, take several years and require visits to Belize at different times of the year to ensure the best chances of finding the indigenous reptiles and amphibians in both wet and dry seasons. I was certainly willing to devote as much time as possible to the endeavor.

To be honest, I was not certain where Belize was located. I had heard several recent news reports about this tiny nation but had no idea it was a mere two hours by air from Houston. Since Belize is only 174 miles long

and 68 miles wide, it is impressive that the country is home to approximately 160 species of reptiles and amphibians.

While it is true that English is the country's primary language, it did
not seem so when I was discussing local herp species with natives. Instead
of more traditional names of snakes, lizards, and frogs, Belizeans use some
downright bizarre names for their wildlife. One of the treefrog species
common throughout the country *(Phrynohyas venulosa)* is referred to as
a "spring chicken." I have no idea why, as it certainly does not look like a
chicken or sound like one. Since its skin is quite toxic, it cannot be eaten
like a chicken.

Many local lizards are referred to as "escorpion," and in no way do they
resemble the animals for which they are named. I will even wager that the
gecko they call the "weatherman" *(Aristelliger georgeensis)* can probably
predict the weather just about as well as meteorologists in the United
States. Other oddities include the striped basilisk *(Basiliscus vittatus)*,
known locally as "cock lizard"; the helmeted iguana *(Corytophanes* sp.),
called "old man"; and the spiny-tailed iguana *(Ctenosaura similis)*, a.k.a.
the "wish-willy." Perhaps the strangest vernacular name of all, "snake waiting boy," is given to a common species of skink *(Mabuya unimarginata)*
that occurs throughout Belize.

Peculiar names are also applied to some local snakes. The brown vine
snake *(Oxybelis aeneus)* is called the "tie-tie" snake; the speckled racer
(Drymobius margaritiferus) is the "Guinea fowl" snake; and the small,
hook-nosed snake *(Ficimia publia)* is referred to as "barber pole." Many
natives generally refer to all snakes as "tommygoff," a name usually applied to their most feared and venomous snake species, the "yellow jaw"
(erroneously referred to as "fer-de-lance"), *Bothrops asper.* The mentality
is similar to that in the United States, where many snakes are referred to
as "rattlers" or "moccasins," whether they are venomous or not.

Belizean town names are also unusual. There is Orange Walk, Young
Girl, Never Delay, Double Head Cabbage, and my favorite, Go To Hell
Camp, to name a few.

• •

Belize airport's diminutive size left me chuckling with amusement. The
entire setup was little more than a modest runway with a small building
that housed the control tower. As our aircraft made its final approach, we
passed directly over an impressive network of waterways that snake their

way through dense jungle. This was my first view of the countryside, and I let my imagination go wild with thoughts of exotic reptiles living in the trees and lining the banks of this most inviting habitat.

As we taxied to the main terminal (actually, the only terminal), I could see several military planes scattered around the landing strip, all marked with British insignia. In addition to the planes, armed British soldiers were in evidence on the tarmac. Unfortunately, this small nation, which gained independence in 1972 (only a dozen years before my visit), is still threatened by its larger neighbor to the west, Guatemala. At the time of my visit, Guatemala did not officially recognize Belize (formerly British Honduras) as an independent nation; as a result, British militia are stationed throughout the country to help keep the peace.

As I stepped off the plane, I was greeted by a wall of thick, damp air that fogged up my glasses and frizzed my already curly, black hair. Although I had lived in Houston for several years (a city which I had believed to be the all-time humidity champion), I had never really known what it was like to breathe water until now.

After undergoing a cursory search through my bags by customs agents, I exited the terminal and was met by Dr. McCoy. He had just said goodbye to one of the Carnegie Museum workers who was on his way back to the United States. After loading my gear into the jeep, we headed to the main campsite, where the rest of the field researchers awaited our arrival. Here I was introduced to other expedition members. This was obviously more than just a herpetological research trip, as I was greeted by several ornithologists as well as a few mammalogists. I could not help notice that one of the mammalogists was picking at a small wound on his stomach. He was preoccupied with this, not even bothering to look up as we were introduced.

"Mosquito?" I asked, trying to initiate some friendly conversation.

"Beefworm!" he shot back in a somewhat irritated tone.

"What the heck is a beefworm?" I asked, at the risk of raising his ire.

"Parasite," was his one-word response. I could not help it, but I was so intrigued that I had to pursue this further.

"Does it hurt?" I asked. For the first time since our introduction, he stopped what he was doing and looked up at me.

"Picture this," he said. "Take a piece of wire, heat it up until it glows red hot, then plunge it into your flesh while you wriggle it around. You think that might hurt?"

After stumbling around camp for a while, I asked Jack if he needed me to do anything in particular. He said no, and within seconds I was a mere speck on the horizon. As I wandered through the tall grass of a nearby field, I occasionally spotted an anole fleeing for cover. Belize has nine varieties of these lizards, but I never collected any of these particular species. I had something more spectacular, more exotic, in mind. I was looking for something on the order of a "Wow, am I glad I invited you on this trip" kind of animal.

I was thinking of heading back when I saw a flash of red in the tall grass ahead. I quickly turned in the direction of the movement but was unable to pinpoint its source. I remained still, and in a moment I saw it move again. This time I could clearly see that it was a snake, although I had no idea what kind. The thick undergrowth made it impossible to see all the way to the ground. I made one feeble attempt to pounce on it, but my effort was so half-hearted that I was certain there was nothing under my cupped hands except weeds. I was right; the snake was nowhere to be seen.

As I wiped the sweat from my face with a cloth bag that I kept tucked under my belt, I glanced down at my feet and noticed a violent thrashing beneath my boots. It was unbelievable; I was standing on the snake. I immediately reached down to grab it but then stopped dead in my tracks. I still had no idea what it was. Although its color pattern was similar to that of some coral snakes, it could also have been one of the harmless coral snake mimics. I was 95 percent sure that it was a harmless species, but I did not want to take an unnecessary risk. Because it was only a matter of time before I either crushed the struggling serpent or it eventually freed itself from under my eight-and-a-half triple-E's, I knew I had to act quickly. Using the cloth bag like a glove, I grabbed the snake at midbody and quickly inverted it into the bag. Peering into the sack, I was finally able to get a good long look at the snake, and I was now 99 percent sure it was harmless.

When Jack saw me back in camp, he asked if I had had any luck on my first outing. "Yep, one snake," I proudly beamed.

"Really, what is it?" he asked. Not knowing exactly what it was, I just handed him the bag, certain that he would blurt out its identity. Peering into the bag, his face lit up with excitement as he exclaimed, "Choice!" (This phrase became his trademark.) "That's one of the prettiest *Micrurus diastemas* I've ever seen." I gulped silently to myself. I had been positive it was harmless. Fortunately, I had taken all the right precautions in capturing this eighteen-inch-long coral snake.

The simple poem that almost everyone learns as a child to tell venomous coral snakes from harmless look-alikes, "Red touch yellow, kill a fellow; red touch black, venom lack," just did not work in this situation. In the United States there are only three species of coral snakes and the poem applies. However, there are more than fifty species of coral snakes in Central and South America, and many of those species displaying "Red touch black" are venomous and can kill you.

••

After planning our itinerary, we stopped in town to stock up on provisions before heading off into the field. While everyone else ran around the marketplace stocking up on "frivolous" things like coffee, tins of fish and meat, fresh fruit, and bread, I rounded up the really important stuff: orange soda, chocolate, and cookies. This was the best I could do, since no shop sold chocolate Twinkies.

In each small town or village we entered, I saw the same disturbing sight. On nearly every street corner was a vendor selling large turtles that either were struggling to right themselves or were tethered by a string attached to one of their rear legs. All were Central American river turtles (*Dermatemys mawii*), an endangered species protected throughout its limited range in Mexico, Guatemala, Honduras, and (supposedly) here in Belize. They have been designated as Appendix I, according to CITES (Convention on International Trade in Endangered Species), which means that special permits are required before they can be collected, studied, or, most importantly, exported from the country. However, as is too often the case, especially in Third World countries, these regulations are seldom enforced against locals who regularly exploit their wildlife, especially when it is used as a food source. In fact, on this occasion, the sale of these turtles was probably sanctioned by local authorities, who themselves partake in the Easter tradition of dining on *hickety*.

A fisherman or hunter walks along the shallow banks of a river or other body of water where a *hickety* can be found and waits for the animal to come to the surface, whereupon he impales the turtle with a pointed stick or spear. After pulling the reptile onto land, he removes the weapon and fills the open wound with sand or mud. This is usually done for cosmetic reasons, as few of the locals are willing to purchase a food item with a bloody, gaping wound. The turtles are then brought to market where they are kept on their backs in the sweltering sun without water, sometimes for days, until they are purchased for the family dinner pot.

I, too, could have eaten a dozen *hickety* turtles every day in Belize without any questions from the authorities. But if I had wanted to capture a single turtle and take it back to the States to perhaps pair it up with another captive one, I would have needed to go through a lengthy, expensive permit request process that would likely have been denied due to the animal's endangered status.

• •

One of the first onerous tasks we faced each time we arrived at a new campsite was to set up mist nets to capture birds. I have assisted with their construction on many occasions, and this has helped me learn a great deal not only about birds but also about people who study them. Mist nets are marvels of technology. They are simple in their concept and design yet versatile in their application and function. The same fragile and virtually invisible net that can capture a bee-sized hummingbird without injury can also trap and incapacitate a 140-pound herpetologist. It is hard to believe that this wispy shadow of material, which looks like a badminton net (only with finer, smaller mesh), has enabled scientists to catch, study, and release birds with relative ease.

A major highlight of each day occurred when the ornithologists came back to camp with birds they had removed earlier from mist nets. Whenever I saw someone walk into camp carrying an armload of cloth bags, I ran to fetch my camera. It was like Christmas. Choruses of "oohhs" and "aahhs" often erupted from the gathered masses once the bags were opened. Some birds were spectacular for their gaudy appearance, whereas others were impressive because of their especially large or diminutive size. What made this ritual of "emptying the bag" so exciting was the endless diversity of birds that were collected. Though we rarely caught the same bird species more than once, these occasional repeat performances did not diminish each bird's beauty in my eyes.

Birds were not the only creatures caught in the nets (present company excluded). Large insects, such as cicadas, grasshoppers, and huge beetles often found their way into these subtle traps as well. Sometimes an insect inadvertently brought about its own demise by attracting a large lizard to the mist net. Once, I witnessed a large male basilisk in the middle of a net munching contentedly on a giant insect, and the next day I observed a giant spider doing the same.

In addition to birds and herps, the tropics are also home to a large array of mammals. We had no mammologist in camp, because their collecting needs took them to a different region of the country. I was nonetheless interested in seeing as many mammals as I could find. I asked Jack if there were many species of bats in this area, to which he replied, "At least several dozen."

"Can we try to catch some? I would really like to get some photos of them."

"Paul, do you have any idea how difficult it is to remove a live, struggling, irritated bat from a mist net?"

"Worse than removing a bird?" I asked.

"Not even close," he said, shaking his head. It really must be quite difficult then, because I watched the crew remove some of the birds from the nets, and I swear, they must practice sewing soap bubbles together to become that nimble and dexterous. If it were up to me, I would cut the bird out of the net each time.

As luck would have it (at least for me), we were late in closing down the nets one night. By the time we visited the last site, we found dozens of bats entangled in one net, all attempting to chew their way out. Several different species were present, each one looking more bizarre than the last. Most were leaf-nosed bats (phyllostomatids), which were adorned

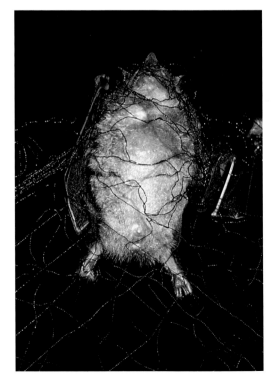

Leaf-nosed bat entangled in a
bird mist net in Belize.

with exaggerated, weird-looking nasal appendages. With flashlights burning dim and bugs biting hard, the group began the laborious task of removing the toothy furballs from the mist nets. The ordeal went rather well. The mist net was only slightly chewed up, we had enough Band-Aids to go around, and I finally got the pictures I had hoped for.

••

My timing for this particular trip was not as well planned as it had been for my previous two trips. It would be at least a month before any appreciable precipitation could be expected. Although the dry conditions would have little effect on the ornithologists, they would severely curtail my work. The absence of rain would mean a paucity of animals, especially snakes and amphibians. Thus, it was in Jack's and my best interest to separate from the birders and meet with them again several days later, allowing us to explore wetter and more varied habitats.

As Jack and I headed down one of the main highways running through the center of the country, we passed a modest lodge whose large green and yellow sign read: "Tropical Jungle Paradise." Beneath the sign was a list of what the establishment had to offer a weary traveler, including private cabins, jungle tours, horseback riding, Mayan ruins, and last, but not least, "hanging out." Jack and I were both amused and intrigued. We decided to stop for a snack and to check out the place as a possible temporary campsite. Proprietor Tom Dale, a young man from New York, had decided to retire to Belize where he planned to live a very "laid-back" lifestyle. When he asked what we were doing in Belize, we told him we were here to collect and study local reptiles and amphibians. He invited us to stay at his facility at a generously reduced rate, because, as he put it, "This place is crawling with wildlife." Since the lodge was on the bank of a river, with good habitat on all sides, Jack and I decided it was potentially an excellent location.

There were twelve cabins in all, none presently occupied. Although Tom's place was clean, it was not very popular. Each cabin had a double bed, but it was far more comfortable to use the large hammock that hung on the porch overlooking the river. Despite the lack of amenities (there was no electricity and everyone had to share a communal toilet), the place had class and charm. Tom went out of his way to prepare special meals for us, and he even let us use his rowboat to hunt along the shore of his property.

One morning I got up rather early, and Tom asked if he could accompany me on a short outing to a wooded area across the river. I was happy

Sign at Tom Dale's place offering all the available comforts in Belize.

to have him along, as I have always lived by the motto "the more eyes, the better," although most times "misery loves company" seems more appropriate. After we climbed the steep embankment on the other side of the river, we had to walk only a short distance to reach a pristine tract of forest where numerous fallen trees lay in various stages of decomposition—a good source of shelter for reptiles and amphibians. We spent the better part of the morning flipping logs and peeling loose bark from numerous trees. Tom really enjoyed this activity, and each time we found something, he wanted to learn everything there was to know about it. When I split open a rotten log and caught a huge night lizard (*Lepidophyma flavimaculatum*) in its center, Tom became really animated. In my haste to catch the lizard, I miscalculated its distance and grabbed it too far back, causing it to lose its tail. When the severed tail fell to the ground and started to wiggle on its own, Tom just stood there speechless, pointing in disbelief at the writhing appendage.

Soon I found another lizard—one I was very pleased to catch. Under a pile of dead palm fronds, I discovered a beautiful adult female elegant gecko (*Coleonyx elegans*), similar to one I had collected a year earlier in Costa Rica but a different species. When I discovered her hiding place, the gecko immediately assumed a threat posture, standing on the tips of her toes in an effort to appear larger and more ominous. Since I wanted to get a picture of her in that threatening pose, I delayed catching her. I cautioned Tom not to move, so that she would maintain that position. My warning was unnecessary. Not only did she stay on her tiptoes after being picked up, but she assumed that position repeatedly over the next two days whenever she was threatened.

By noon we were back at the lodge, where we showed Jack the day's catch. He nodded in approval, uttering the "choice" word several times. After the show-and-tell, Tom prepared lunch before we took our obligatory midday siesta. These breaks were not due to any fatigue on our part, but they kept us from burning to a crisp in the steamy afternoon temperatures that frequently soared above one hundred degrees.

Without fans to stir the breeze, we found it nearly impossible to fall asleep in the oppressive heat. After I had finally nodded off, I was irritated to be awakened sometime later by Tom's voice, asking if I was interested in capturing a small lizard that was moving about on the end of my hammock.

"Tom, you're hallucinating, it's over a hundred degrees now. There is no way a lizard would be foolish enough to be out in this heat," I whispered back. Just to humor him, I put on my glasses and glanced at the end of my hammock. I was surprised to catch a brief glimpse of what I thought was a lizard's tail disappearing behind the pole holding up my bed. I quickly scrambled over to the post to see if it was indeed a lizard. Sure enough, walking around the base of the hammock, completely oblivious to every-

Jack McCoy holding a tiger rat snake, one of the many snakes we found in Belize.

one, was a two-inch-long gecko *(Sphaerodactylus glaucus)*. Although its coloration was mostly light gray, the underside of its tail was bright orange, and it elevated that tail in display as I tried to catch it. After securing the lizard, I tried again to get some rest, but on such trips, rest is something I had learned to live without.

By sunset, Jack and I were anxious to try our luck at road cruising. Due to its diminutive size, Belize does not have many roads to choose from, so we ended up driving down the only road at our disposal, the "Hummingbird Highway." At no time was the effect of the drought more significant in terms of finding snakes and amphibians than during road collecting. Even on a "bad" night under wetter conditions we could expect to find several species of frogs and toads and perhaps a snake or two; but without rain, we had absolutely no luck at all.

Now and then we saw what appeared to be some kind of animal on the road ahead of us, the sight of which gave us a brief rush of anticipation. But each time we approached these objects, we nearly always found them to be birds—more specifically pauraques, pronounced poor-ah-keys *(Nyctidromus albicollis)*, a species closely related to nightjars and whippoorwills. Like these other nocturnal aerialists, pauraques have relatively small beaks and enormous mouths, which in flight they fill with mosquitoes, moths, and other flying insects.

Seeing literally nothing on the road for nearly two hours, we became discouraged, but finally we had a break. Yelling "snake" and slamming on the brakes, I flew out of the car just in time to intercept a snake nearing the edge of the road. With Jack's help, I bagged the eighteen-inch-long yellow jaw tommygoff *(Bothrops asper)* and carefully placed the bag far in the back of the jeep. We definitely did not want any accidents to happen while blindly reaching back for something to eat or drink. With their inch-plus-long hypodermic fangs, most pit vipers can easily bite through a cloth bag and envenomate a careless handler.

The rest of the night was disappointing. Except for another small tommygoff, which was badly squashed, we saw only a treefrog that bolted across the road before we could stop to catch it. Although it was not the most productive night, we were pleased to have caught at least one snake—and thankful it was not an eight-foot-long adult.

The next morning I was up early trying to figure out how to photograph the viper without being bitten or allowing it to escape. The solution was simple. I placed the snake in our ice chest for several minutes until it was cool enough to be safely manipulated. However, instead of concentrating on photographing the snake, I was now distracted by the wonderful smells emanating from the kitchen, and soon I found myself with fork in hand and a mouthful of the fluffiest scrambled eggs I had ever eaten.

"More eggs, Paul?" Tom asked, after my third helping.

"No, not for me, I don't eat breakfast," I explained. At that point, I remembered what I had initially intended to do before I got sidetracked. I jumped up from the table and ran over to the ice chest.

"Damn it," I bellowed, as I opened the ice chest. The pillowcase that contained the snake had fallen and was now submerged under three inches of ice water.

"Problem?" Jack asked.

"I just killed the *Bothrops*." I was hoping to keep it alive to bring back to the States, as I had promised a colleague that I would save him any live pit vipers I came across. On the bright side, I no longer had to worry about the snake escaping or biting me while I tried to photograph it. I carried it by hand to a small clearing near one of the huts. Placing the reptile in various "naturalistic" poses, I took several photographs that I thought made the snake appear to be alive. (This is a common technique I have used on many expeditions and is referred to in the business as "nature faking.") Following the photo shoot, I returned the snake to the cold, soaked bag, tied a knot in it, and hung it on a nail in the main dining room for Jack to preserve. Half an hour later, Jack removed the bag from its perch, untied the knot, and poured the contents on the table. Before grabbing the snake, he gave it a long, hard look, then turned and gave me a long, cold stare. The "dead" snake was flicking its tongue as it slowly crawled off the table.

Two days later, another herper wanted to photograph the snake, but since the viper had had time to recover, I decided it would be safer if once again we cooled it down first. After nearly forty-five minutes in the cooler, I was both astonished and extremely upset with myself to discover that, once again, I had killed the snake. This time, however, I was careful not to use my hands during the photo session, just in case we were dealing with some kind of supernatural snake. The precaution was well founded. Several minutes after the "dead" snake was exposed to the warm environment, "Lazarus" was once again among the living. This was one snake I was not going to turn my back on and would never again try to photograph. Despite the failed attempts on its life, the snake survived the trip to the United States. It was welcomed by my colleague who, after hearing

Yellow-jawed tommygoff *(Bothrops asper)*, "Lazarus," collected crossing the road on Belize's Hummingbird Highway.

the story of its miraculous recoveries, made sure it was kept in a double-locked, escape-proof cage.

••

After we had spent a few days at "Jungle Paradise," it was time again to rendezvous with the ornithology team at a quaint little resort on the Macal River. Although Chaa Creek was nothing more than a few modest bungalows bordering a deserted stretch of forest, it nonetheless had a tremendous amount of ambiance. Owned by Mick and Lucy Flemming, this tiny oasis was a breath of cool, fresh air in an otherwise hot, dank environment. The Flemmings' gracious hospitality, combined with their fantastic culinary expertise, made our stay here a truly memorable experience.

In addition to the handful of simple, well-kept bungalows, a large central building doubled as the main dining area and gathering place for those who wanted to spend their time exchanging stories of the exquisite wildlife they had encountered at the resort.

Jack and I were directed to put our gear in one of the larger huts, which two of the bird researchers, Scott and Bob, had occupied the day before. Accommodations were simple but functional, consisting of three beds on the main floor and another upstairs in a small loft. I requested the upstairs bed, and since no one else wanted to climb constantly up and down stairs, my wish was unanimously approved. Besides, the others felt that their nightly toilet run could be hampered by a nearly fifteen-foot fall to the ground.

While we dined on one of the finest home-cooked meals we would eat during our stay in Belize, we filled each other in on events of the past few days. It was wonderful to have a bellyfull of good food and to be so exhausted that despite the ridiculously hot nighttime temperatures, we fell asleep as soon as our heads hit our pillows.

The next morning I was up early and raring to go, but despite high hopes of seeing every herp species in the area, I was able to find only a single anole and a couple of insects—rather humble pickings indeed.

I returned to camp to drop off my "massive" catch and to ask Jack if he wanted to join me for some "real" herping. After finding a rather sizable stand of palm trees, many of which were in various stages of decomposition, we began the task of raking through the fallen, dried palm fronds in search of wildlife. Under a pile of decaying leaves, I uncovered a somewhat nondescript, three-inch-long scorpion. Despite my great interest in scorpions, I discovered that this one was just a blackish brown run-of-the-mill arachnid. I turned away from the scorpion and continued to rake through the debris. A moment later, I felt a sharp, burning sensation on the back of my neck. Instantly my hand found the source of the pain. The scorpion had apparently climbed up the back of my boots and onto my pants, then eventually made its way to my shoulder. The pain was both immediate and intense. I called out to Jack for help, but he was out of earshot. Not knowing which species had stung me, I was not sure if I should try to make it back to camp for help or sit down in the shade of a tree and make out my will. Instead, I decided to catch the scorpion and ask Jack to identify it.

"Nice, *Centruroides pococki*. . . . Choice."

"*Centruroides?*" I gulped. I immediately recognized the genus as the same one that occurs in Arizona: the only species in the United States that can be lethal to humans. (That species is the sculptured scorpion, *Centruroides sculpturatus.*) "Is it dangerous?" I asked, almost not wanting to hear the answer.

"Not unless you're an insect," he replied. Jack had a way about him that with very little effort could turn anyone's anxious moment into a smile and a sigh of relief. In a few minutes, both the pain and the scorpion were gone.

In addition to the scorpion, there was an abundance of other wildlife on this ridge. After turning over every last piece of debris, we ended up with two red coffee snakes *(Ninia sebae)*, a small eight-to-ten-inch-long harmless species; a juvenile elegant gecko *(Coleonyx elegans)*; and a "*Peripatus*"—the latter a most unusual creature, sometimes referred to as a velvet worm. This creature is so different from any other animal that for

Belizean scorpion *(Centruroides pococki)* that stung the author in the neck.

years scientists could not even agree on which *phylum* it belonged to. Although it superficially resembles a caterpillar, it is not an insect nor is it an annelid worm. It is classified as an onycophoran, presumably a missing link between arthropods and annelids. There are about 120 species of velvet worms, mainly in the world's tropical regions, ranging in length from a few inches to nearly one foot long. The one I found was just over two inches long. Although not much to look at and certainly not very menacing in appearance, *Peripatus* has evolved an effective defense to deter would-be attackers. When molested or touched, these animals "spit" a noxious and sticky fluid that, on contact, can leave a small animal incapacitated and in severe distress. I observed this firsthand when I initially picked up the animal and watched it squirt a minute thread of clear, viscous liquid onto my fingertips. I felt how sticky it was, and I realized how

An odd invertebrate, the "velvet worm," in "midspit"— eastern Belize.

difficult it would be for an insect, spider, or even a small vertebrate to gain the upper hand in a confrontation with such a formidable foe.

I took it back to camp, hoping to capture its defensive act on film. If you think photographing a two-inch-long, constantly moving animal is easy, try getting it to "spit" on command. But patience has its rewards. After many hours of trying, I was fortunate to capture on film a *Peripatus* in midspit.

By late morning, when the temperature soars into the upper nineties and the humidity is not far behind, it is too uncomfortable to be in the field looking for specimens. Thus, I spent the rest of the day photographing an endless parade of beautiful birds that had been snared in mist nets. Species diversity was staggering. In a few hours, I had exposed half a dozen rolls of film on such birds as collared trogons *(Trogon collaris)*; masked tityras *(Tityra semifasciata)*; white-fronted parrots *(Amazona albifrons)*; and a most interesting bird, the tiny, five-inch-tall ferruginous pygmy-owl *(Glaucidium brasilianum)*. This species is also known as a "four-eyed" owl due to distinct markings on the back of its head which resemble large, black eyes. Such a "face" makes potential predators think twice about trying to sneak up on this small raptor.

Throughout the day, more birds were caught in the mist nets, their beauty nearly beyond description. When we first removed one specimen from a holding bag, it seemed rather plain looking. However, after quickly surveying its surroundings, this robin-sized bird erected a crest of brilliant red feathers, the upper margins of which were tipped with an absolutely gorgeous fluorescent blue. When it got its bearings, it swayed its head from side to side and opened its mouth to expose a bright yellow interior—an impressive sight. This bird's common name suits it well: the royal flycatcher *(Onychorhynchus coronatus)*.

Royal flycatcher *(Onychorhynchus coronatus)* displaying its brilliant head crest after having been removed from a mist net in Belize.

Crimson-collared tanager *(Phlogothraupis sanguinolenta)* showing what is perhaps the most vivid red coloration in the animal kingdom.

Yet, the bird that most enamored me was the crimson-collared tanager *(Phlogothraupis sanguinolenta)*. This seven-inch-long species is jet black except for the majority of the head, neck, throat, rump, and eyes, which were the most vivid red I had ever seen in the animal kingdom. Adding to its stunning overall appearance is its silvery white beak, which stood out in stark contrast to the vibrant red-and-black plumage.

My main regret is that I could take pictures of a bird only while it was in someone's hand; the animal would have escaped, of course, if it had been perched in a more naturalistic setting. This meant I could photograph only the bird's head and neck; any more would have revealed the handler's hand or fingers. I vowed that if I ever were invited on another such expedition with ornithologists, I would devise a way to photograph these animals more appropriately. (Ultimately I did; see chapter 5.)

With a few hours to wait before the evening meal, I went out into the bush to search for insects and spiders to feed to the elegant gecko I had captured a few days earlier at Tom Dale's place. In Belize, or anywhere else in the tropics for that matter, you do not have to go far to find invertebrates, so in a matter of minutes, I returned with a container full of culinary delights for my traveling companion. I placed a few of these in the large Styrofoam container that housed the gecko and returned after dinner to check the box to see if the gecko had eaten. When I opened the container, all I found inside was a solitary insect but no lizard. It was obvious the insect did not eat the lizard; it must somehow have escaped. But how? On closer examination, I discovered that the plastic handles on either side of the Styrofoam box had fallen off, exposing two large holes big enough to allow the lizard to crawl through. I searched every detail of the cabin, lifted everything off the floor, and looked inside every bag, shoe, and container, but to no avail: the lizard was gone. Great. I had promised a friend I would bring him this specific animal for his research project, and now I had lost it. Needless to say, the whole ordeal depressed me. I spent the rest of the evening walking around the bungalow with my flashlight, hoping to find the little "ulcer maker."

Feeling discouraged, I climbed into the upper loft to sleep. Before long, something caught my attention. Flying and hovering above me was what appeared to be a pair of tiny car headlights. However, without my glasses on, I could have mistaken an avocado for a vacuum cleaner. Yet, within arm's reach was some type of creature that was releasing a tremendous amount of bioluminescence. I eventually caught it and was especially pleased that I had accomplished my mission without causing serious bodily harm either to myself or to this strange aerialist. My catch did not have the same effect on the rest of the crew as it did on me, but their lack of enthusiasm did not diminish my own exuberance at having caught this marvelous creature.

Jack told me that it was a click beetle, similar to the lightning bugs we have in the States, although they are in different families. These, however, were unlike any fireflies I had ever seen back home. Their bodies were about three times the size of those of their northern cousins, and instead of lighting up periodically, these elaterids (the family of insects to which they belong) stay lit for as long as it remains dark.

Like a child who has collected fireflies, I placed the insect in a small jar and walked around in the dark using my "living" flashlight as a would-be night-light. I was so impressed by the brightness of this single insect that I just had to find a way to translate this phenomenon into a photograph. By using a tripod and placing the bug in an open container, I was able to take several long exposures that yielded excellent results.

With my spirits high again, I drifted off into a deep and peaceful sleep—sleep that would soon be interrupted by a most dramatic and bizarre event.

Just after 3:00 A.M., I was awakened by slapping sounds, followed by murmuring voices and a barrage of flashlight beams piercing the darkness in every direction. Putting on my glasses, I called down to ask what all the commotion was about.

"Army ants," was the unified response, "millions of them!" At first I thought it would be best if I remained in the loft and stayed out of harm's way. Then I realized that I was probably needed downstairs to assist the others with moving our gear to safer ground and helping to remove the ants. It was truly an awesome sight. There were literally millions of ants

A click beetle photographed in a cup using a thirty-second exposure (and no flash) in Belize.

on the march, and it appeared that their path took them directly through our bungalow. All the stories and movies about massive ant swarms marching through the jungle and devouring anything too slow to get out of their way now took on a whole new meaning for me. Watching this scene, I realized there were only two choices when encountering these six-legged marauders. Get out of their way or die.

As we observed from a safe distance using our flashlights, we occasionally caught a glimpse of some unfortunate creature being chased out from under the bungalow by the hoard of ants. In addition to two red coffee snakes, several other herps were attacked, including the female elegant gecko that had escaped earlier. Except for a few stubborn ants still clamped to her skin, however, she was in good condition. Another victim was especially significant, although we did not confirm this until we returned to the United States. It was about two feet in length and was later identified as a species of slug-eating snake (*Sibon* sp.). It also had several ants imbedded deep in its skin, and it appears it would not have survived except for our intervention. Jack picked the ants off the snake and studied it carefully. Although it looked to me like the common slug-eating snake (*Sibon nebulata*), Jack thought otherwise. He instructed me to take several detailed pictures of the animal, so we would have good photographic documentation just in case the snake managed to escape. When I asked what he thought it was, he said he was not sure but that it might be a species of slug-eater known from only a single specimen. Jack was right. The snake proved to be an obscure species *(Sibon neilli)* known from a single example found many years ago in the capital of Belize in—of all places—a pharmacy, where it had been kept in a bottle of alcohol without any specific locality data. This particular species has since been classi-fied as a subspecies of the pygmy slug-eating snake, *Sibon sanniola neilli*.

About a year after its capture, Jack wrote a brief article in one of the herpetological journals about our snake's amusing rediscovery, noting in the acknowledgment section that he wished to thank the column of army ants for their assistance in its capture.

••

Overall, the trip was a success. The museum added valuable new speci-mens to its permanent herpetological and ornithological collections. There was already talk of another expedition the next year to continue the on-going research in Belize.

My return to Houston marked a noticeable change in my overall be-havior. I was restless, and I had difficulty concentrating on my day-to-day activities. I was certain my problem was depression brought about by the fact that I was home when all I really wanted was to be back in Belize. I assumed that in a few days I would return to normal (whatever that was).

Several more days passed before I discovered the real reason for my irritability. On top of my head was an area that had become more and more sensitive to everyday activities such as brushing my hair or putting on a shirt. The cause of the discomfort, however, was not yet clear. With each passing day, the pain became more intense. Since the location of the pain was directly on top of my head and because I have rather thick, bushy hair, I was unable to see exactly what the problem was. I finally relented and asked my friend Debbie if she minded having a look at my scalp.

Rare slug-eating snake *(Sibon sanniola neilli)* that was forced out from under our bungalow in Belize by a giant column of army ants.

After carefully examining the area, she reported the presence of several pimplelike structures. I found it hard to believe that I was nearly incapacitated by a couple of zits.

By the next day my head hurt so badly that I could not even endure a light breeze blowing through my hair. This was getting ridiculous. I could not begin to imagine what was going on up there, but then it suddenly dawned on me. I immediately called the Carnegie Museum and asked Jack if my symptoms could be those of an unwelcome visit from Mr. Beefworm.

"Sure sounds like it to me," Jack said. I then asked if anyone else on the expedition had been experiencing the same problem. "No, not that I'm aware of," he said sympathetically. "I think you're alone on this one." The best advice he could offer was that I see a doctor and explain what I might have been exposed to in the field.

Unable to eat, drink, or sleep, I was in no condition to report to work. For the first time in my five years of employment at the zoo (and the only time in the twenty plus years I have spent on the job), I was forced to call in sick. As much as I wanted to avoid it, I could no longer put off the inevitable—I was doctor bound.

Before leaving for the doctor's office, I asked Debbie to take another look at my head. She said she could see several small furrows of dried, caked blood that resembled miniature crayfish holes, from which trickles of fresh blood would ooze periodically. I asked her to *gently* try to clean away the dried blood so that a clear view of the "problem area" could be seen. This was by no means a simple task, and as soon as I was peeled off the ceiling, I was on my way to the doctor's office.

After trying to explain my dilemma to the nurse at the HMO clinic, I was finally able to convince her to call in a doctor to examine me. Forty-five-minutes had passed before an elderly physician entered the room reading the nurse's report. Without even looking up, he asked me if there were any of these "worms" that he could take a look at. I told him there were several on top of my head and one on my neck just behind my right ear. He briefly glanced at my head then wrote out several prescriptions for me to have filled. And just like that, within thirty seconds, he was gone.

Out of desperation, I went to the nearest pharmacy to have my prescriptions filled. I was somewhat puzzled by the doctor's choice of medications. One was an antihistamine, one was a weak painkiller, and I am not exactly sure what the third one was, but to this day, I cannot have children. Needless to say, my condition worsened, and I subsequently discontinued taking the medications. As the pain became unbearable, I was still no closer to finding an answer to my problem. I had no choice now but to do the unthinkable—go to a specialist.

As I knocked on the dermatologist's door, I began to have visions of numerous electrodes protruding from my shaved head, sending high voltage shocks to the area in an attempt to barbecue my little beefworm companions. I was relieved, however, when a calm, pleasant-looking gentleman asked me into his office to explain my problem. He listened intently to my story until I spoke the magic word: beefworm. At that point, he jumped up from his chair and lunged for one of his medical textbooks on the shelf behind him.

"*Dermatobia hominis*. I can't believe you have them, that's *fantastic*. This is so exciting to me," he said. "You see, I read about this back in 1958, and I never thought I would actually get to see one except in a book. I don't suppose you still have any of them on your person?" he inquired.

"Well, as a matter of fact I do, and I'll make you a deal," I told him. "You remove them from my head, and you can keep them for yourself." As tempting as that was to the doctor, he explained that this whole issue was beyond his expertise, and all he could do was recommend a specialist in tropical medicine. I thanked him and made my way over to the Baylor School of Medicine.

I told the nurse at Baylor that I had recently returned from an expedition to Belize, Central America, and that I might have been parasitized by a beefworm.

"Beefworm," she said excitedly. "Stay right here." In a moment, three doctors surrounded me and began to poke and prod at my head.

"It appears that you're right," one of them said. "It does seem to be some sort of parasite."

"With your permission, we would like to attempt to remove them," another doctor said. He did not have to ask twice. In a matter of minutes I was lying face down on an operating table while scores of doctors crowded the room carrying cameras and small glass vials. After several injections of anesthetics into my scalp, the doctors began digging around in my skull with their scalpels.

"We got one," one of the doctors said excitedly. "It's pretty small but it's definitely a *Dermatobia*." All the doctors then gathered around the vial containing the tiny invader to get a better look. Before it was all over, they had removed six worms from my head.

"Hey guys, do me a favor," I asked before they finished stitching up my head. "Save me one of those things so when I retell this story I'll have some proof that I'm not completely out of my mind." So, armed with a small glass vial and its strange-looking occupant, I made my way home, triumphant that I had endured a most harrowing and exhausting experience and thankful that it was all over.

A couple of days after surgery, I occasionally felt a slight twinge of pain coming from the general vicinity of where the parasites had been removed. I tried to dismiss it until one time when the pain was so severe, I jumped to my feet and screamed, "They're back, someone get them out—*now!*"

Sure enough, when I went back to the doctor's office a week later to have the stitches removed, they found another beefworm.

Great I thought, now I have to go through the pain and expense of another surgery, but the doctor was quick to offer me an alternative.

"You know, Paul, since this whole ordeal started, I've been doing some reading on this subject, and I've found what I believe to be a painless and simple solution to your problem. Since this parasite is fairly common and widespread in the tropics and since most of the indigenous people can't afford to pay a doctor to remove them, they often solve this problem simply by placing a small piece of meat on top of the parasite's burrow. This ultimately causes the worm to suffocate, during which time the parasite tries to bore into the meat, thereby exiting the human host."

I stared intently and silently at the doctor, waiting for him to burst out laughing. Of course he had to be kidding, but his facial expression never changed. He was totally serious.

"Do you expect me to believe that story?" I asked in disbelief.

"Paul, I sincerely recommend you give it a try. If it doesn't work, you can always come back and have the surgery."

At one time or another, everyone has stood in front of a mirror to prepare for a big night out or an important date, but I will wager that few people have had to watch themselves tie a piece of meat to their heads in the hope of enticing a beefworm out of their scalp.

With my head held high (and motionless) and my dignity as low as it could be, I remained frozen in position for several hours. Later that evening, I convinced Debbie to come over for what I hoped was the final check on my status. The look on her face was priceless when she entered the room and saw me sitting there with meat strapped to my head. Her demeanor changed, however, when she carefully untied the cloth that held the chunk of meat balanced so precariously on top of my head. Slowly, she lifted the meat off my head until she was able to determine what progress, if any, the parasite had made. With remarkable calmness, she

Larva "beefworm" *(Dermatobia hominis)* removed from the author's head sits on the piece of meat used to "entice" the parasite from its hiding place.

explained that the worm was indeed half-buried in the now soggy, smelly piece of steak.

"Quick, grab it before it changes its mind!" I yelled to her. She rapidly flung the beef from my head and with a small pair of forceps grabbed the parasite midbody and pulled it from its burrow. We both cringed as we heard the faint popping sound it made as its body tore away from mine. There it was: a half-inch long nightmare complete with several rows of black spines encircling its body, designed to make it nearly impossible to dislodge the larvae from its host. I stared at the creature in awe. On the one hand, it was the most repulsive thing I had ever seen, but as a scientist, I certainly could appreciate its place in the scheme of life. Unable to take my eyes off the worm, I did what any dedicated biologist-photographer would do: I shot an entire roll of "Wendy" (my nickname for "her," from the popular commercial of the time when "Where's the beef?" was at its height).

I thought my ordeal was finally over, but I was wrong. As Debbie was cleaning up the wound on my head, she noticed yet another beefworm inhabiting a spot next to the hole vacated by "Wendy." By this time I was so exhausted and traumatized that I was not about to sit still for several additional hours with another slab of meat perched on my head. Debbie concluded that since the meat worked (probably because it acted as an asphyxiate), then some other substance, such as a thick hand cream, might work as well.

I applied a small glob of hand cream to the area where the remaining beefworm resided. In about twenty minutes, the last parasite made its way up through the layer of cream, and I was finally free of these most unwelcome tenants.

My retelling of this experience has affected different people in different ways: some are amused; others turn away grimacing in absolute horror. Personally, I cannot wait to return to Belize.

• •

Since my involvement with the beefworm, I have read a great deal about this unusual animal. This parasite, which is sometimes referred to as a botfly, primarily infects cattle and other large domestic hoofstock. It is considered a serious pest because of the damage it causes by burrowing into the skin of its host (there can be sometimes over several thousand individuals per animal), rendering both the meat and the hide unusable.

This particular species, *Dermatobia hominis,* has an interesting life cycle. The adult, which is actually a fly, catches a female mosquito in midair and cements four to ten eggs to its abdomen. The mosquito, in turn, lands on a warm-blooded animal (usually cattle, but sometimes dogs and even humans) whose body warmth soon causes the eggs to hatch. Tiny larvae immediately burrow into a host's skin and remain there for up to six weeks, during which time they continue to grow as they feed on the host. When the worms are about half an inch long, they emerge from the host's flesh, fall to the ground, and enter a pupal stage, during which they complete their life cycle by metamorphosing into adult flies.

Another way a beefworm can transmit its offspring to a host is to place its eggs on the abdomen of a tick. Like a mosquito, a tick searches for a warm-blooded host on which to feed, passing the hatchling larvae on to the unsuspecting animal. As I often had ticks all over my body because of my frequent forays into wooded and grassy areas, I most likely was infected in this way.

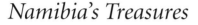

CHAPTER 4

Snakes, Scorpions, and Scorching Sands

Namibia's Treasures

THE PROGRAM FIRST AIRED in 1977. It was perhaps the most influential television special I had seen up to then. The show was National Geographic's "Living Sands of the Namib." It was narrated by Burgess Meredith, whose eloquent voice had me mesmerized and sitting on the edge of my seat. Filled with wondrous sights and sounds, the program transported me to one of the most desolate places on earth, the Namib Desert in the southwest African nation of Namibia (then known as South West Africa).

I have always been partial to deserts, having spent several years of my youth in the deserts of the Middle East and, in more recent times, conducting herpetological surveys in the southwestern United States. The images I was now seeing on TV were unlike anything I had seen before: lizards that "swam" beneath oceans of sand and diminutive nine-inch-long vipers that buried themselves under the sand with only their eyes above ground. There were unique chameleons that spent their entire lives on the ground in search of desert beetles, geckos that "barked" at their prospective mates in hopes of luring them into their underground burrows for mating, and so much more. These incredible sights were not just confined to herpetofauna: images of plants, insects, birds, mammals, and especially of the breathtaking scenery were all stunning. By show's end, I vowed that I would someday make the journey to this faraway place to experience for myself this magical desert.

Nine years later, I decided I could wait no longer. I spent nearly a year writing letters and communicating with others who either had been to Namibia or knew about the country. My question to each was simple: what was the best time of year to visit Namibia to view the greatest diversity of herps? Only one of a dozen people queried responded with specific information. His answer was simply, "May and June." Based solely on that response, my travel plans were to be in Namibia in May and June of 1986.

Preparing for such a venture was mind-boggling: checking the type of malaria medication required, identifying local languages, finding maps, obtaining pertinent herpetological field guides, and researching relevant collecting and exporting laws. I also had to learn about weight restrictions on personal baggage and even what is considered "pornographic" material (and the penalties for being caught with such items). Consequently, any field guides that showed hemipenal morphology or reptiles copulating were left behind. Yet perhaps the most important bit of information I needed was the Namibian word for chocolate. (Yes, I am an *international* addict.)

For six months prior to my trip, I corresponded with Dr. Hartwig Berger-Dell'mour, an Austrian herpetologist at the Windhoek Museum in Namibia. Hartwig (pronounced Hartvig) offered to help me in every facet of my herpetological expedition while I was in Namibia. He graciously met me at the airport, allowed me to stay at his home, obtained the appropriate collecting and exporting permits, and even took time off from his work to show me the best collecting sites in the country. Without Hartwig's assistance, I would have accomplished very little.

• •

Before I left Houston, a friend built two large wooden crates in which I could transport all my equipment to Africa. I hoped to fill them with reptiles and amphibians before returning home. I specifically chose to have them made of wood, so that the collecting bags (full of reptiles and amphibians) could be nailed to the sides of the crates, ensuring they did not fall onto each other and cause injury to the animals during transit.

The crates turned out to be huge monstrosities with a tiny wheel on each corner and numerous air holes along the sides. Weighing about forty-five pounds each (empty), they were so large and bulky that they could be maneuvered only with considerable effort by two people. By airline rules, each piece of luggage could not exceed seventy-two pounds, yet here I was with two pieces of luggage that were more than half the weight restriction—and they were still empty. After numerous repacking sessions and several trips to the airport to weigh the crates on the airline's scales, I finally managed to get the crates to the limit of seventy-two pounds each. (I actually had to file some wood off one of them.) At the time of my departure, the crates were placed on the airport scales and, at exactly seventy-two pounds, met the weight requirements.

However, I was still not out of the woods. As I checked in for the final leg of my journey in South Africa, a woman at the ticket counter informed me that I must pay a penalty for my "oversized" luggage. Confident I was in the right (and also having a copy of the airline regulations with me), I suggested she check her rule book again to verify I was not over my limit. She nodded in agreement about the weight aspect but explained that my luggage had exceeded the 203-centimeter rule and therefore was considered oversized. I was mortified. I had taken all precautions regarding weight limits but had given no thought to size limits. She informed me that I was quite fortunate that I had not been charged the penalty for the previous leg of my flight, as it would have exceeded the cost of my plane ticket. She went on to say that if I planned to bring these crates back with me to the States, I should expect to pay a very large penalty fee. Needless to say, the crates never left Namibia.

My layover at the Jan Smuts Airport in Johannesburg was overnight. As I tried to corral my two giant "albatrosses" onto the puny airport cart, I asked a woman at the information booth if there was a place I could lock up my belongings until my departure the next morning. She pointed to a large room and said she would find someone to unlock the door to allow me to deposit my things there. She then asked me which flight I was leaving on the following morning. When I gave her the flight number, she informed me that the flight had been changed from 8:30 A.M. to 10:00 A.M. I thanked her for her help and left the airport for a nearby hotel.

It was late in the afternoon when I checked into my room. Despite the difference in time (South Africa and Namibia are seven hours ahead of EST), I was too excited to sleep. By 9:00 P.M. (2:00 P.M. my biological time), I was getting tired but still could not sleep. The television was not much help since there was only one station available (this was not merely a hotel restriction; that is all there was in South Africa and Namibia). I finally got to sleep at 7:00 in the morning, which gave me only ninety minutes of rest. By 8:35 I was at the information booth requesting my luggage. When the clerk asked for my flight number, I told him that I was going to Windhoek. He then said in a low, apologetic voice, "Sir, that flight departed just five minutes ago."

"What?" I shouted. "That's not possible! I was told the flight was changed to 10:00 A.M."

"Who told you that?" he asked. I explained that the woman who was sitting in that very chair gave me that information, and her name was Beth. "Well, I'm sorry sir, but she gave you the wrong information. That flight leaves every morning at 8:30." He told me that the next flight out was at 5:00 but that it was full, so I would have to catch the 8:30 flight the next morning.

I shot him a look that could have killed his children. He said he would look into the matter and do everything he could to get me on the 5:00 flight. Meanwhile, I telephoned Hartwig and advised him that I would not be arriving as scheduled. He chuckled knowingly and said he would meet me later that evening at the Windhoek airport. Fortunately, I had no other delays.

• •

My arrival at Windhoek's airport was routine. Within seconds, a man walked up to me and asked if I was an American researcher named Paul Freed. I smiled, warmly extended my hand, and said, "Hartwig, it's a pleasure to finally meet you." When he saw the volume of luggage I brought with me, he asked me if I was moving to Namibia permanently.

We used the forty-five-minute ride back to his house to get to know each other, but I was too distracted by the blacktop to pay close attention to what he was saying. After all, I was finally in Namibia and excited about seeing my first herp cross the road. Noticing my preoccupation with the road, Hartwig asked what I was looking for. I told him, "Herps, naturally."

He laughed and said we would not see any herps out at night since this is not the right time of year for night collecting.

"What do you mean not the right time of year for night collecting?" I asked in an almost hostile tone. "I was told that the best time for visiting Namibia to collect reptiles and amphibians was right now."

He said we would certainly see a fair share of the indigenous herpetofauna at this time of year, but it was by no means the best time to collect herps in Namibia. For that, I needed to be here in December and January—their summer. This discussion was to become a recurring theme between us and something he would repeat many times during my monthlong stay.

By the time we arrived at his home, I could see why night collecting was going to be problematic; it was in fact damn cold. Hartwig advised me not to be overly concerned, as we would still find some interesting herps, even in the cold, and that the farther north we traveled the warmer it would get.

After introducing me to his wife and children, Hartwig showed me to the guest room and told me to make myself at home.

"You get a good night's sleep; we have a long month ahead of us, and it starts early tomorrow morning in the permit office," Hartwig said before calling it a night.

••

The drive from Hartwig's house to the permit office the next morning was a short one, but for me it was an eye-opening experience. I was expecting a gravel or dirt road passing nothing but sand dunes as far as the eye could see. Instead, we drove on a four-lane super highway (on the left side of the road—England's contribution to the region) through downtown Windhoek, where tall office buildings and high-rise apartments dominated the landscape. On almost every street corner was some reminder of life in the States: Teller II machines, Toys "R" Us stores, Kentucky Fried Chicken stands, and more. Somehow, perhaps as a result of watching various television programs, I thought that Namibia (and even all of southern Africa) was an impoverished and desolate area without electricity, where people lived in tents and had never seen an automobile. I could not have been more wrong.

At 9:00 A.M. we showed up at the permit office to meet with Mike Griffin, an American biologist in charge of herpetological research in Namibia. I had been corresponding with Mike for several months prior to my trip, during which time I had outlined to him my research proposal. Mike, a former Californian, had lived in Namibia since the early seventies and had a keen interest in and knowledge of the local birds and small mammals as well as the herps of southern Africa.

When we were introduced to each other, Mike was sitting behind his desk. Without taking his eyes off me, he reached under his seat and pulled out a large burlap bag. As we talked, he untied the bag and pulled out a three-foot-long dwarf python *(Python anchietae),* which he then handed to me. My eyes opened wide and I excitedly asked, "Is this my welcome-to-Namibia present?" Mike laughed and said, "No, this is one of several specimens of this species that are brought to my office each year." I explained to Mike that the Houston Zoo, where I currently worked, had the only specimens of this species in the Western Hemisphere and that the zoo snakes were successful in reproducing. He was not particularly impressed, and despite my further insistence on trying to secure permits to acquire these pythons, the answer was still a definite no. I asked Mike how common these "Angolan" pythons were in Namibia. (This is the common name we use in the United States for this species.) Before answering, he expressed his displeasure at my referring to them as "Angolan" pythons. While they range into southern Angola, he explained, they are no more common there than in Namibia. I sensed a point of contention here and wanted quickly to smooth any feathers I might have ruffled.

"How do you refer to them here?" I asked.

"We call them dwarf or anchieta's pythons." Okay, no problem, I thought.

"So, how common are they?" I asked again.

"Well, they certainly aren't as rare as *Python sebae* [(the African rock python)]." His response took me by surprise since rock pythons are very common in public collections as well as in the pet trade, whereas dwarf pythons have never been commercially available. (Some U.S. zoos and private collectors have put a price tag of ten thousand dollars on a single dwarf python.) He then went on to explain that each year the public brings to his office four or five dwarf pythons, compared to only one or two rock pythons. I tried one last time to broach the subject of collecting permits for dwarf pythons. Mike must have been in a good mood. Instead of throwing me out of his office, he said that perhaps in the future, if I could adequately justify the reasons for wanting dwarf pythons, he would consider granting a permit. He did say that captive breeding was not enough justification. In the end, he leaned over and whispered that even if he gave me the necessary permits, there was very little chance of my encountering a dwarf python in the wild.

I then asked him what and how many specimens I would be allowed to collect. I explained that a particular species designation was not important to me. Since I was conducting a survey on parasites in herps in general, what I really needed was a "blanket" permit to collect whatever species of reptiles and amphibians I might encounter. He shook his head and said that was highly irregular; blanket permits are not authorized. After a brief discussion, he reconsidered and presented me with a collecting permit for ten examples of each species native to Namibia. However, there were a few restrictions. Nine species of herps were classified as protected and therefore not to be collected. They included the two aforementioned pythons, the two species of monitor lizards (Nile and savanna), and the five indigenous tortoise species. Furthermore, I could not collect in any national park or other protected area. In spite of these restrictions, I was ecstatic. I now had permission to capture up to ten specimens of nearly 250 different species.

When I asked Mike about good places in the field to collect, he described one area in particular that sounded almost too good to be true. It was in central-eastern Namibia, where years earlier a long cement canal had been constructed to transport water to remote, arid regions from the wetter areas in the northeast. This canal, about 120 miles long, four feet deep, and three feet wide, winds through some remote regions and inadvertently traps all manner of wildlife in its deep trough. Unfortunately, while constructing the canal, no one had thought to include a cement "curb" on either side of it, which would have prevented many of the desert animals from falling into this oversized U-shaped "gutter." Although many of the animals were caught at night, some fell into the canal during the day. This structure did not discriminate among mammals, invertebrates, or herps (occasionally, even some birds were found); nor was the animal's size a limiting factor. There are even reports of giraffes and gazelles having been found in the canal, dead or with broken legs or necks. The canal is nearly always dry, except when water is intentionally "sent" through, thereby hastening the demise of animals unfortunate enough to have fallen in. With summer daytime temperatures soaring well above one hundred degrees by late morning and without structures to provide shade, a trapped animal quickly succumbs to the intense Namib Desert heat. Many animals could have been saved if there had been steps or other such irregularities in the walls that would have provided a foothold for their escape.

According to Mike, it might be possible to find seldom-encountered herps like tiny blind snakes (Leptotyphlopidae), thread snakes (Typhlopidae), or even mole vipers (*Atractaspis* sp.) in the canal. That casual comment had me on the edge of my seat.

"When do we leave?" I asked excitedly.

"*We* don't," he replied, then went on to explain that Namibian authorities are well aware of how the world in general views stories regarding animal atrocities and that such negative publicity would be devastating to Namibia. I asked him how such reports would get out into public domain, and he said through people like me who are armed with cameras and notebooks. I assured him I had no intention of revealing any such compromising situations. As a show of good faith, I told him that I would be willing to leave all of my camera equipment behind. He appreciated the gesture but felt that he could not take a chance.

To my disappointment, I had to settle for a few herps that had been collected recently from the canal by museum staff members. It turns out that as part of their normal job duties, several museum staff members regularly drive up and down the length of the canal to remove any stranded wildlife they encounter. They note this activity in a detailed log describing the species collected, whether the animal was alive (and subsequently released), or whether it was found dead and later preserved for the local museum. In this logbook, which I was permitted to examine, I noticed the tremendous diversity of wildlife species that had become statistics for this "killer canal," as it has recently been referred to by the media. I mention the whole issue of the canal only because several stories have since appeared in print, which brought this matter to the attention of the public. I certainly would not have betrayed the confidence that Mike Griffin asked me to keep if it were still unknown.

• •

After consulting a map, Hartwig and I decided on an ambitious route that would take us on a lengthy journey through most of central and southern Namibia. Our adventure began not far from the capital on a mountain range that includes one of Namibia's highest peaks, Mt. Moltkeblick. At eighty-two hundred feet (over twenty-five hundred meters), it certainly is not the talk of the mountain-climbing circuit, but it is not just a walk in the park either. Our climb to the top was hampered by numerous dolomite rock cliffs that cut our hands and shredded our shoes. Also making it difficult and uncomfortable was the seemingly endless array of bushman arrow plants that sprouted from every crevice and rock on the mountain. With each step we took, these plants left their diminutive spines in our pants, shoes, and skin. Though I hoped Hartwig would not consider me a whiny wimp, I was compelled several times to ask him what it was that occurred only on this mountain that justified going through this hell. He assured me that we would see something here that I would see nowhere else in the world. He was referring to a species of girdled lizard *(Cordylus pustulosus),* which is endemic to this mountain range. Of the half-dozen species of girdled lizards found in Namibia, this is the rarest and most difficult to find.

The climb took the better part of the morning, and I was glad we were not attempting this challenge in December or January (summertime). Along the way, we encountered several herp species of which I had never heard. One gecko species in particular which is quite interesting is the festive gecko *(Narudasia festiva).* At two to three inches long, it is one of the smallest geckos in Namibia, but unlike most other indigenous geckos, this one is diurnal and very agile. It spends most of its time among rocks and boulders, where it hunts ants and flies. Another unusual saurian found here is the dwarf-plated lizard, *Cordylosaurus subtessellatus.* This small, slender relative of the girdled lizards has a bright blue tail that, as in many other lizard species, breaks off if touched or handled, then twitches and wiggles to distract predators, thus giving the lizard a chance to escape. Of three we collected, only one had an intact tail.

By the time we reached the summit, I was winded, but as much as I wanted to rest, I did not want Hartwig to think I could not keep up with him. Actually, I could not. Even though we were almost the same age, he was in much better physical condition. After turning over several hundred rocks and coming up empty-handed, I asked Hartwig to describe the size and basic coloration of this endemic lizard. He reached into a cloth bag that hung from his belt and pulled out several of these rare animals, saying, "They look like this." Here I was, stumbling around, moving a sizable portion of Namibia one rock at a time, and he had already caught three of the lizards. This was only one of the many times Hartwig would demonstrate his superior skills when it came to finding and catching local herpetofauna.

Despite the strong blowing wind and the approach of evening, I was not about to leave the mountain without having caught at least one of these elusive lizards. It took a while, but finally, by observing the size, location, and type of rocks under which Hartwig caught his specimens, I finally captured two of these unique Herero girdled lizards.

Hartwig was pleased with our first outing into the field; he was also impressed with my performance and perseverance. Although many scientists visited him in Namibia to collect local reptiles and amphibians, none wanted to climb Mt. Moltkeblick due to the extreme physical demands. I felt a sense of pride, and more than that, I felt that I was beginning to earn Hartwig's respect.

It sounded incongruous to me, but in fact Namibia was punctuated with hundreds of farms and farmers, and it seemed that Hartwig knew them all. On one such visit to a friend's farm near the capital, Hartwig and I tried our hand at finding an unusual and most interesting species of lizard. Although the lizard is not particularly spectacular either in size or appearance, its behavior is quite remarkable. At hatching, the bushveld lizard *(Heliobolus lugubris)* is only about two inches long, and its coloration is mostly black with several white spots and white lines scattered along its back and head. When confronted by a potential predator, the lizard demonstrates an unusual defensive behavior. Raising the rear portion of its body high in the air, it locks the hind legs rigidly and walks in a stiff, jerky manner, rocking from side to side. To me, the bluff just did not seem that threatening. To other indigenous fauna, however, it appears to be a real and serious threat. Occurring sympatrically with the bushveld lizard is a species of beetle (*Anthia* sp.) known locally as an "oogpister" ("eye squirter") that when provoked or attacked raises its rear end in the air and rocks its body from side to side. If the antagonist continues to attack, the beetle squirts a pungent, acidic fluid directly into the attacker's face. Although not lethal, the experience is so unpleasant that few animals care to try their luck a second time. Though many animals mimic the behavior or appearance of others, this particular example is rare, as it is one of only a few known instances of a vertebrate species imitating the behavior of an invertebrate. After several months, when the lizard is half-grown, its coloration gradually changes to that of the adult, in which the white spots fuse into white lines and most of the black coloration becomes gray or brown. At this stage in its life, the lizard no longer mimics the eye-squirting beetle in either appearance or behavior.

Adult and juvenile bushveld lizard *(Heliobolus lugubris)* showing the difference in coloration between the two. Juveniles mimic the eye-squirting beetle in coloration and in the way they walk.

Eye-squirting beetle or "oogpister" (*Anthia* sp.) can repel a predator with a noxious fluid sprayed into the face of an attacker.

After observing the lizards, I made several attempts to catch them. I wondered why they rely on this unusual behavior when they move so quickly that it seems nothing can possibly catch them. If I *felt* foolish trying to catch these lizards, I only had to look at Hartwig to realize that I *looked* foolish as well. He was quite amused watching me do this bizarre "jig," in which I went through a series of abrupt 180-degree turns, all the while trying to slap my hand down on these elusive, two-inch-long Houdinis.

He then returned to the vehicle and came back carrying one of the telescoping fishing poles he had asked me to purchase for him back in the United States. While he prepared this secret weapon, I tried again to best him by catching one of the lizards before he could. This time, I brought out one of my "big guns," an oversized rubber band. I had had some successes in the past using these stun devices to catch large, fast-moving lizards in Central America, but given the size of my "prey" here, I put little faith in this technique. But I had to try. Not wanting my first attempt to be a failure, I applied a little too much force as I tried to gently "stun" the young bushveld lizard I was pursuing. Consequently, when I approached Hartwig triumphantly with my prize in hand, he asked, "So Paul, what species of *leg* is that?"

Hartwig then showed me the proper and skillful way to catch these fast-moving lizards. Using a piece of nylon fishing line that he fashioned into a mininoose, he secured the line to the end of the telescoping rod. Not being much of a fisherman, I had never even heard of a "telescoping" fishing pole, so when I actually found such a device in a sporting goods store back in the States, I was most intrigued by it. Although I was quite sure that the manufacturer never intended it to be used to catch lizards in the Namibian wilderness, I was amazed by its usefulness.

After Hartwig spotted a lizard, he extended the fishing pole until the tip and attached noose were directly over the target. I soon discovered that a lizard usually tolerated minor disturbances nearby—such as a dangling fishing line—as long as I was at least ten feet away. Hartwig then carefully maneuvered the noose over the lizard's head and around its neck just in front of the forelegs. Once he positioned the line, he quickly yanked the pole skyward, and the weight of the lizard caused the fishing line to close down around its neck—capturing the surprised lizard unharmed. Hartwig was like a surgeon, skillfully placing the noose over his subject's head and, time after time, effortlessly catching even the most elusive lizard. I was especially impressed that he could perform this feat no matter what the circumstances. He snared lizards that were virtually enshrouded in vegetation, he was able to approach even the most skittish of lizards, and he could slip the noose over the head of a lizard despite a fierce wind that often prematurely closed the noose or entangled it in a nearby bush.

At this snaring technique, Hartwig was truly a master. He insisted I also give it a try, but I visualized the outcome even before making my first attempt. In the first place, my eyesight is not that good, so to lower a half-inch noose over the head of a small lizard ten feet away and jerk it up at just the right moment is not within my means. In spite of this, I did try the noose a few times. I suppose one of the reasons Hartwig and I got along so well was that I must have been a great source of amusement to him. No matter how hard I tried, I could not capture a lizard by using this technique.

We continued to hunt in the area until late afternoon, then headed back to the main farmhouse. On the way, we passed through a field littered with large termite mounds, a common sight throughout much of the region. On occasion, I used my snake rake to rip open termite mounds, since a variety of lizards and snakes frequently live inside them. Most of the time, however, it was impossible to penetrate these sunbaked fortresses, but even when I was successful, the mound was usually empty, having long been abandoned by its owners. Occasionally, I found a small gecko or lacertid lizard in one of them, but it was my hope to find a snake or perhaps a clutch of snake eggs incubating inside. Once, while I was examining a three-foot-tall mound, Hartwig called my attention to some movement in the nearby brush. Straining to get a glimpse of what appeared to be a large snake heading straight toward me, I asked Hartwig, "Is that a cobra heading my way?"

"No," was his excited reply, "it's a mamba, and you're standing in front of its house. Get out of its way—*now!*" I quickly stepped away from the front of the termite mound and watched as this nine-foot black mamba *(Dendroaspis polylepis)* disappeared down a small hole at the base of the mound. Although I was probably in no real danger (as long as I did not prevent the snake from gaining access to its burrow), I still felt that my encounter was a little too close for comfort. I asked Hartwig if it would be possible to dig the snake out of the burrow, but he just smiled, shook his head side to side, and continued on his way back to the farm.

The owners of the farm were expecting us and were in the middle of preparing a sumptuous dinner. Since it was still light out and since I was still in a herping mode (which is the case essentially all of the time I am in the field), I asked permission to walk around the farm in search of herps. There were no objections, so I went outside to the barn. In a matter of minutes, I was able to find a fair number of the ubiquitous Bibron's gecko *(Pachydactylus bibroni)* and a couple of speckled geckos *(P. punctatus)*. Behind the main barn, I noticed a patch of earth that looked as though it had been under water previously, but which was now cracked and dry from exposure to the sun. I returned to the house to ask if in fact there had been standing water in that area at some time. Mrs. Fischer, the farm's co-owner, explained that she had planted a modest garden there, and each time she finished watering it, she noticed a small temporary pool formed from the runoff. I asked whether I might dig around the area to search for any frogs or toads that might have burrowed down to escape the harsh, dry season. She laughed and said, "Help yourself."

Within five minutes, I unearthed my first frog—a golf-ball-sized "sand frog" *(Tomopterna cryptotis)*. Thirty minutes later, I bagged my limit of ten frogs, some from as deep as two feet underground. Hartwig was in disbelief.

"You can't find frogs this time of year!" I heard him mutter this expression three more times during the ensuing month, but I never got tired of hearing it.

The day ended with a superb meal consisting of two kinds of antelope (kudu and oryx), which, I might add, tasted nothing like chicken.

The following morning, Hartwig and I drove to another farm not far away where the surrounding hills were covered with many flat rocks, ideal habitat for several species of girdled lizards. This farm was a much larger farm than the first one we had visited. Shortly after our arrival, the farm owner told his workers to be on the lookout for any lizards or snakes they might encounter. After turning over countless rocks for several hours, Hartwig and I returned to camp to find that one of the men had caught for us a fairly stout, six-foot-long cobra *(Naja haje anchietae)*. The dead snake was placed in a coiled position at the door to our bungalow. Since I could not have properly preserved such a massive reptile without using up all my formalin, I decided to keep only its head as a voucher specimen. (Sometimes even just a portion of an animal, such as the head or skull, can be valuable as a museum specimen, especially from an obscure species or from a region seldom explored.) After cutting off the snake's head just behind the neck, I noticed something protruding from its throat: it was the tail of another snake. Surprisingly, it was another cobra of the same species that measured just under five feet in length. Apparently, this species is cannibalistic and is capable of eating a meal nearly equal to its own body length. Since this meal must have been eaten several days earlier, it was too decomposed to be salvageable as a museum specimen.

Despite our modest success in capturing reptiles and amphibians in this region of the country, I felt that I had not yet experienced the true essence of herping in Namibia. After all, we had not encountered even a single sand dune; nor had I seen a single herp species depicted in the National Geographic show that was my reason for being here. After pleading with Hartwig to "head for the sand," he finally consented, and we were on our way to the small seaside town of Lüderitz in the southwest corner of the country.

En route, Hartwig occasionally pulled off the road to search the barren landscape for holes in the ground. I watched him pass numerous holes until he found one that must have appeared slightly different—although to me they all looked alike. With a small hand trowel he carefully dug into the ground, making sure that he always had some portion of the hole in sight. After following the winding burrow into the soil for several feet, he used his hands to gently dig away the loose sand until he exposed a small and bewildered gecko. When he found one of these geckos on his first attempt, I thought he was the greatest magician alive. He calmly reached down, picked up this tiny jewel, and handed it to me. I was now holding one of the three endemic barking, or whistling, geckos *(Ptenopus garrulus)*. It was a good thing this lizard did not jump toward my face, because with my mouth hanging wide open, I would have, without a doubt, swallowed it whole. When I finally was able to speak again, I asked Hartwig if it would be possible to catch adults of this species.

"What do you mean?" he asked in puzzlement. "This *is* an adult."

This lizard was only three inches long, and I thought they reached about six or eight inches. My estimation was based on the large image I had seen in the National Geographic special in which the entire head of the gecko filled the television screen.

I was still in such awe of what I had just witnessed that I had to see if it was luck or skill.

"Can you do that again?" I asked.

Without much fanfare, Hartwig proceeded to study the various holes in the earth and again stopped at one he thought would yield a gecko.

Pointing to a hole virtually identical to the one he was kneeling over, I asked him why he had skipped over this one.

"That one has a beetle in it," was his prompt response. While Hartwig began to dig out the hole he believed to contain a gecko, I proceeded to work on the one he claimed was occupied by a beetle. Before I was half finished with my excavation, I noticed Hartwig had his second gecko in hand and was watching me in amusement. Finally, a small, dark tenebrionid beetle scurried out of the hole I was digging and immediately began to look for a place to hide.

To me, the holes were identical, but to Hartwig's trained eye my hole had the slightly domed appearance indicative of a beetle and was not the hole of a gecko.

"Okay, now you find one," he ordered. After a few seconds' search, I pointed to an appropriately shaped hole.

"No, that one is a scorpion hole," he said smiling. "You can tell by the flattened shape of the hole."

"How about this one?" I asked.

"Now you've got it; that's a gecko hole," he said reassuringly. After removing several feet of substrate and losing sight of the hole twice, I concluded that this burrow was unoccupied. When I stood up to search for another hole, Hartwig asked me why I had given up.

"There's nobody home," I said.

"You better check again," he replied. He then knelt over the hole and proceeded to find the opening that I had inadvertently caved. Using his fingers, he carefully scratched away until he found the burrow that split into two separate paths. He followed one path until it dead-ended. He then backtracked and followed the other path until it led him to another gecko. This one was a male, which is characterized by a bright yellow patch on its throat. At this point, what could I say except that Hartwig really knows what he is talking about. After several more failed attempts,

I finally got the hang of it and was able to collect a few of these elusive lizards myself.

Since we could not reach our destination in one day, we decided to camp before darkness fell. Hartwig knew his way around Namibia quite well, so he had us make camp in a seldom-visited area that was actually in a dry riverbed. This river, the Kahn River, except for very infrequent rains every few years, has almost no water anywhere within its borders.

We managed to set up our tents next to a small temporary pool just before the sun disappeared behind a large mountain chain. Whenever I am out camping, I try to find some source of water because animals often migrate to such wet places. I really never expected to find any such treasures in this remote and barren spot, but as darkness fell, and I switched on my flashlight, I noticed a small, shiny, jumping object on the edge of the pond. Once again, I was successful in finding the "unfindable" frogs. In a matter of minutes, I had caught a series of yet another type of "sand frog," *Tomopterna marmorata*.

Later we decided to investigate the riverbed near the rock walls to search for geckos. As it was early June—winter in Namibia, since seasons are reversed from those in North America—the temperature became chilly as soon as the sun went down. I still had lingering doubts that we would find any reptiles or amphibians in such cool weather, but by now I should have learned to trust Hartwig's instincts and his knowledge of the local fauna. As we approached a large rock face, we converged our flashlight beams on an eighteen-inch-long snake that was about to escape beneath a giant boulder. For the first time since my arrival, Hartwig became excited and very animated.

Although I had never seen a living one, I did recall seeing photographs of this unusual snake, *Pythonodipsas carinata*. Its common name, western keeled snake, is inadequate to describe this marvelous serpent. Although its scientific name alludes to the snake's superficial resemblance to members of the python family, it is not at all related to the pythons, and despite its flattened, wedge-shaped head, neither is it a viper. It is instead a colubrid (the family of snakes that includes most serpent species), and it is found only in portions of Namibia and southwestern Angola. This primarily nocturnal reptile spends much of its time in and around rocky areas, hunting small lizards. Its enlarged rear fangs deliver a mild venom that subdues its small prey. This venom is very weak and not harmful to humans. In the beam of our flashlights, the snake's elliptical pupils were reduced to tiny slits, while its tongue rapidly flicked in and out as if it were in search of answers concerning its capture. Although catching it was easy, I knew keeping it alive until my return to the States would be more difficult.

We bagged the snake and made our way to the high, rocky wall. Our lights occasionally revealed a gecko making its way across the large, smooth rocks. The lizards were extremely alert and at our slightest approach climbed well beyond our reach. We failed to catch even a single gecko.

As morning broke, I returned alone to the rocky area to try to redeem myself. With the help of several large rubber bands and some tools to pry the rocks apart, I finally succeeded in catching three of these Namib day geckos *(Rhoptropus bernardi)*. However, by using rubber bands, I broke the tails off two of the lizards. Moments later, Hartwig came by with his fishing pole in hand and proceeded to catch half a dozen geckos within a few minutes, all with their tails intact.

Faced with a long drive, we broke camp and headed southwest. Here, the blacktop roads were excellent, long straightaways that stretched for many miles into vast, seemingly barren desert. At one point, I noticed a foot-long lizard ambling slowly across the road. When I finally slowed our vehicle enough to get a good look at it, I nearly dove out of the car while it was still going twenty-five miles an hour. There, in the middle of the road, was a Namaqua chameleon *(Chamaeleo namaquensis)*, blending in so perfectly with the blacktop that it was virtually invisible. I grabbed my camera and took its picture before it could change color or had a chance to wander off the road. Curiously, it appeared that nothing in the area offered suitable shelter or even a place to escape the heat. There were no bushes or trees to climb, only sand and gravel. Hartwig explained that Namaqua chameleons escape both heat and predators by digging bur-

A Namaqua chameleon *(Chamaeleo namaquensis)* is virtually invisible as it crosses a remote highway in western Namibia.

rows in the ground. They are voracious predators capable of eating several dozen beetles at one time. They have also been known to prey upon other small lizards and snakes.

Sadly, their superb camouflage occasionally leads to their death. Too often, while basking in midday sun, they are squashed by cars. This is especially true for gravid females that utilize the hot road surface as a kind of thermal "blanket." This daily road basking ultimately helps them by raising the incubation temperature, thereby assisting with the development of their unlaid eggs.

Although the road has little traffic, chameleon mortality must at times be high. During one hour of travel on this road, we found six dead chameleons, four of which were loaded with eggs. In addition, we caught five others alive.

• •

Approaching Lüderitz, we watched the coastal fog roll in over the tall dunes and slowly engulf the enormous expanse of endless sand. Even thirty miles away, we could differentiate the thick white clouds from the pale yellow dunes. Since rain is almost nonexistent in this region of Namibia, the flora and fauna rely largely on these fogs to provide them with life-sustaining moisture.

Hartwig guided us to a row of bungalows at the edge of Lüderitz Bay. Overlooking the water were a series of small, private rooms with kitchen facilities and hot running water that allowed us to relax in comfort and style. Hartwig was a little apprehensive about the cost of such a luxury, but I assured him I could afford it. Our twin room cost five dollars a night.

Since we were both very hungry after our long drive, we made the local restaurant our next stop. Befitting that of a seaside resort, the menu was loaded with descriptions of countless goodies from the sea. In addition to having a large variety of fish, the restaurant touted their shrimp and lobster as the best in the country. I happen to be quite fond of fish but never really had much taste for shellfish. I told Hartwig to feel free to order anything he desired, including the lobster dinner. I was rather surprised by his response, considering the fact that he was a well-traveled person.

"I've never had lobster; I don't know if I would enjoy it," was his humble reply.

"You've never eaten lobster?" I shouted across the table, just loud enough to embarrass him. "Well, then lobster it shall be." Hartwig looked at the price of the meal and began to protest strongly.

View of the massive dunes near the coastal town of Luderitz in southwestern Namibia. Note our vehicle in the center of the picture for scale.

I looked at the price, did a quick conversion to U.S. dollars, and smiled, saying, "It's okay, Hartwig, you are worth the four dollars."

I must admit, for four dollars I did not think he would get much of a meal, but when the waiter brought out three good-sized lobsters, I knew it was an unbelievable bargain. Before Hartwig was halfway through his dinner, I knew he had become a shellfish addict. I excused myself from the table for a moment and after finding our waiter, I instructed him to bring another order of lobsters to our table. The look on Hartwig's face when the second plate of lobsters arrived was the same as I had when I found the Namaqua chameleon crossing the road. This place was unreal. You could live like a king here and still not break a twenty-dollar bill.

The huge meal, combined with the long drive and the coastal air, made me extremely tired. I suggested to Hartwig that instead of roaming around the desert this evening, we turn in early and get a good night's sleep. First thing in the morning we would attack the dunes, fully refreshed. He agreed, and within minutes we were both fast asleep.

The next morning, after a quick, light breakfast, we drove out of town to a spot where Hartwig had done some collecting during the past year. Just a few miles outside of Lüderitz the great sand dunes covered nearly the entire landscape. As a result of the strong coastal winds that blow in from the western bay, the ever-shifting dunes are constantly eroded and reformed. Some reach the incredible height of more than one thousand feet—the highest sand dunes on earth. To me, this was a magical place. And despite Hartwig's ribbing that I came at the wrong time of the year, I was glad to be here now. In June the mild winter temperatures are only 85 to 90 degrees; December or January's sweltering daytime temperatures can exceed 140 degrees.

One species of lizard that I wanted to collect in Namibia is found only in the sand dunes of this arid, inhospitable place. It was made famous by the National Geographic television special that shows the animal raising its feet off the scorching sand by simultaneously lifting its left front foot and right rear foot, then alternating to lift both its right front foot and left rear foot. Unfortunately, it was just not hot enough for us to observe first-hand this unusual behavior. However, we did catch a few of these shovel-snouted lizards *(Meroles [Aporosaura] anchietae)* as they came out from under the sand to search for small insects on the surface of the dunes. Curiously, they also eat seeds and plant detritus that collect on the sides of the dunes. When first pursued, these three-inch-long lizards run across the soft sand at remarkable speeds. While it was possible to keep up with them on level ground, I found the lizards were completely unapproachable as they scampered up the steep dunes at top speed. Trying to race up a hill at a sixty degree angle on soft sand while sinking up to your calves (all the while diving after these zigzagging acrobats) is a most humbling experience. The only real chance of capturing the lizards occurred when they dived into the sand, and we were able to see exactly where they burrowed. We could then scoop up a large section of dune, grasp the lizard once it was exposed, and place it into a container before it could wiggle free.

In some areas, dunes come right down onto the beach, where they are continually pounded by ocean waves. Here it was not difficult to find signs of human encroachment. There were many tracks left in the sand by dune buggies and motorcycles as well as a more typical sign: household garbage. Tin cans were strewn along the beach, most of them well rusted from the saltwater. At one point, I picked up a rusted can, intending to dispose of it properly, but was startled when I heard a scratching noise inside. Suspecting that it contained a small animal of some kind, I placed the opening inside a clear plastic bag and then vigorously shook the can. A second later, a spotted desert lizard *(Meroles suborbitalis)* was scurrying around inside the bag. Obviously, the lizard had crawled into the can to absorb the heat created by the sun's rays, thus warming itself much more quickly than if it had lain out unprotected on this cool morning. I combed the beach for additional cans, collecting two more lizards from a total of eleven cans. Under some circumstances, garbage apparently does have its uses.

Hartwig had brought with him several dozen pitfalls that he intended to set up in and around some of the vegetated dunes. They were of simple design, consisting of a funnel-like metal lid with a two-inch hole in the center, which is then placed over a small plastic container buried in the ground. The premise is that a small animal, preferably a lizard or small snake, will walk or crawl across the smooth surface of the lid and then fall into the container below. The lid prevents the animal's escape. Under harsh conditions, such as during intense heat or heavy rains, we frequently checked the traps to prevent an animal from overheating, drowning, or possibly escaping. At this time, we checked our traps twice daily.

It was an adventure to peer into the traps the first thing each morning, like opening gifts at Christmastime. We were never sure what we might find. More often than not, the traps were empty, but on several occasions we caught prize specimens. Most of the captures were lacertid lizards (*Meroles* sp.) and skinks (*Mabuya* sp.), although we caught a few snakes and geckos as well. When he sets these same traps in December and January, Hartwig often catches the tiny Peringuey's viper *(Bitis peringueyi),* considered one of the smallest venomous snakes on earth. Like the sidewinder rattlesnake of the southwestern United States, the Peringuey's viper moves sideways across loose sand. Unfortunately, we found none of these nine-inch-long beauties during my stay in Namibia.

While our traps did some of the work for us by day, we spent many hours at night searching the dunes for specimens. On a particularly cold night, as we drove from one dune area to another, I noticed something small walking across the dirt road in front of the car. I stopped just as Hartwig jumped out to capture a very angry and squawking giant ground gecko *(Chondrodactylus angulifer),* a species I had seen only in books and on television but never alive in the field. I was so thrilled with finding this lizard, I immediately asked if there were a chance to collect additional specimens.

"If it were January, you could find hundreds of them," Hartwig said. This was another reminder that I was here at the wrong time of year. I had barely put the car in drive when I thought I saw something else near the front left side of the car. Hartwig got out of the car and momentarily disappeared beneath it. When he returned, he held his closed hand over my two hands until he saw that I was ready to receive his prize. Then he opened his fist. The experience of having this nearly translucent, pink, bulging-eyed lizard land in my hand was like being handed a million dollars.

"*Palmatogecko!*" I screamed. Of all the animals I had seen on the National Geographic television special, this was the one I wanted to see more than any other. If I could choose only one lizard to take back to the States

A web-footed gecko (*Palmatogecko rangei*) collected at night on a sand dune when the temperature was only forty-four degrees Fahrenheit.

with me, it would be this one, the web-footed gecko. It was unlike any lizard I had ever seen. Three inches long, it had huge eyes that were mostly black but with a narrow red line on either side of the slitlike pupil. Its feet were all webbed (hence its common name); with these it burrows into the shifting sand to escape the intense desert heat. Its body was nearly see-through, and when it was sprayed with water, the lizard lapped the droplets from the top of its head and its eyes with its long, thick tongue. I was most surprised by the fact that the last two lizards we collected were out foraging when the ambient temperature was only forty-four degrees. It was also fortunate for the web-footed gecko that we happened by just when we did. One of the favorite meals of the giant ground gecko is tender, succulent, web-footed geckos.

• •

My stay in Namibia was rapidly coming to an end, but there was still much to do in the next five days. In Windhoek, I would need to apply for animal export permits, for which I began to prepare a list of the animals we had caught. This was no simple task; when the final tally was made, we had recorded nearly three hundred herps. (We actually caught many hundreds more than this, but released the majority back to the wild.) Not all the specimens we had collected would be returning in my luggage; some would become part of the Windhoek State Museum collection. During the daylong drive back to the capital, I badgered Hartwig into allowing me to take all the rare, unique, and unusual herps back to Houston, and his response was more than fair. He gave me ninety percent of the collection and even promised to send me additional specimens later.

The drive back was long but certainly not boring. After passing through the dune region, Hartwig took a short detour to show me one of the most unusual and interesting plant species on earth. It was the rare, endemic Welwitchia plant *(Welwitchia mirabilis)*, the only representative of its family and one of the oldest-known organisms. Some of these plants are more than fifteen hundred years old. While a large specimen appears to have numerous long leaves trailing from the main body of the plant, in reality, it has only two broad, thick leaves that split and curl as the plant grows. Since water is so scarce in this desert region, the two leaves act as a surface "sponge," absorbing water droplets from the periodic fog. Thus, Welwitchia can sustain itself for years without the benefit of rain.

In the south-central region of the country, we passed through an area where the soil is rich in iron and other minerals, resulting in vibrant red and orange dunes that glowed brightly in the late afternoon sun. As we drove past the dunes, we saw a small group of oryx antelope in the distance, climbing one of these beautiful mountains of sand. I asked Hartwig to stop so that I could try to photograph this breathtaking scene, but it was a futile effort. No sooner did I exit the vehicle than the oryx bolted; within seconds they were completely out of sight. Disappointed and frustrated, I took a single picture of their tracks in the red sand as a reminder of the moment. When I returned to the car, I noticed three ostriches on the opposite side of the road. They, too, were quite some distance from us, and before I could even point my camera in their direction, they were off. When I asked Hartwig why everything was so easily spooked, he said he suspected that poaching might be the cause of such behavior—even way out here.

By observing the map, I could see we were not on a direct route back to Windhoek. Hartwig wanted me to meet someone. A short time later we pulled up to a long, white wall with the letters "DERU" written across it.

"What does it stand for?" I asked.

"Desert Ecological Research Unit," he answered.

"So, who lives here?"

"Dr. Mary Seely lives and works out of this facility," Hartwig explained. Meeting *the* Mary Seely, of National Geographic fame, was a bonus I did not expect. Even to the very end, Hartwig continued to surprise me.

Dr. Seely was in the middle of some work but quickly put it aside when we entered the compound. We chatted for about an hour as if we had been friends all our lives. Dr. Seely has been instrumental in organizing and guiding entomological research in Namibia since the late 1960s. She has been involved in an ongoing scientific project studying the life histories of the tenebrionid beetles in the deserts surrounding the research station.

••

The next few days in Windhoek were hectic. In addition to permit matters, shopping, and last-minute photography, I had my hands full feeding and watering all the newly acquired herps.

One of the few luxuries I allow myself while on these trips is the acquisition of some kind of trinket—preferably herpetological in theme—to serve as a reminder of the trip. And, while Windhoek certainly had its share of gift shops, it was sorely lacking in reptile and amphibian artifacts. My needs aside, I was hoping to find a special gift to give to Hartwig for all his hard work, his gracious hospitality, and especially for all the time he had sacrificed in helping make this the trip of a lifetime for me. What could I possibly give this man that would express my thanks for taking three weeks from his busy work schedule, keeping him apart from his wife and children, driving five thousand miles throughout Namibia, giving me nearly all the animals we collected, securing necessary wildlife permits, and letting me eat every ounce of chocolate in his house?

I looked long and hard in all the shops for something befitting this special man. In each shop, clerks would ask if they could help me find something in particular. Each time I explained that I was looking for something unusual—something out of the ordinary. Without exception, each clerk offered me the same thing: ivory. As a guest in their country, I certainly did not want to appear rude, so I fought the urge to yell at them for their blatant disregard for the law. On two occasions I did point out that the sale of ivory is universally against the law without specific permits. Each time I went through my speech, I was told that it would be no extra trouble to print up whatever document I wanted. In fact, most salespeople stated they would even leave a blank spot on the form where they are instructed to indicate the amount of ivory sold (and its year of acquisition) just in case I wanted to buy more somewhere else.

On the day of my departure and after much soul-searching, I found that the best gift I could give to Hartwig had been under my nose the entire time—my camera. During my entire stay, Hartwig had been admiring my camera gear, and while I did not have anything that was state of the art, the two Canon A-1's I had were several steps above the broken-down, fifteen-year-old camera he was using. As we said our goodbyes, I first handed him the camera manual. He looked at it blankly and thought that perhaps there was information in it that would be applicable to his own camera. He extended his hand for me to shake and thanked me for the thoughtful gift.

"No, no, Hartwig, that's not the gift; *this* is the gift," I said as I pulled the camera from behind me. As I got into the taxi that would take me to the airport, Hartwig extended his hand once again, shook his head, and said, "Crazy American, have a safe trip home."

The plane ride from Windhoek to Johannesburg took no more than an hour. Now, however, I had a seven-hour layover before the long flight to New York, so instead of rotting in the airport, I decided to take a bus into downtown Johannesburg. So I would not have to carry my camera bag with me, I stored my belongings in an airport locker. After five hours of downtown shopping, I finally made my way back to the airport with a single package under my arm. I was fortunate to find a curio shop that had numerous animal carvings including a nice one depicting a crocodile, three feet long, with its mouth half-open to expose numerous sharp teeth. Now my trip was complete. I had forty-eight rolls of exposed film, two large ice chests bulging with herps, and my carry-on croc.

As I stood in line to board the plane, I noticed a lot of people paying close attention to small portable radios and anxiously reading the front page of the local newspaper. Thinking it was just a sporting event, I did not give it a second thought. When I finally reached my seat, a flight attendant came by and asked if I would like a newspaper to read. When she handed me the paper, the cause of all the commotion became clear. Less than six hours earlier, riots had broken out in downtown Johannesburg, and a state of emergency had been declared. While I wandered through the streets of Johannesburg, the apartheid protests had just been unfolding. Headlines announced that anyone caught in the downtown area with a camera would be arrested and jailed. I sat in my seat trembling and very thankful that I had decided to leave my backup camera at the airport.

••

Thirty-one hours had passed from the time I left Hartwig's house until I had landed in Houston. I had not slept, and to make things worse, the customs agent in New York had made me show him every animal in both ice chests. The experience had been extremely nerve-wracking. Finally, after landing in Houston, I went to the baggage claim to pick up my belongings, but to my horror I discovered that one of the ice chests was not there. Why is it that it is always the most important item that is lost or stolen? Why couldn't it have been the bag with my dirty underwear? I asked an airline employee where the missing piece might be, and the individual told me it had been sent on by mistake to San Antonio. After I insisted that it be returned to Houston immediately, the employee asked me what was in the bag that was so important that it had to be returned so quickly. I realized that the airline would not take too kindly to my transporting dozens of venomous snakes, lizards, and other life-forms, so I told the attendant, "You know, clothes and stuff."

The next morning I arrived at the airport at 6:15 and walked through the empty terminal to the baggage claim area. There, to my delight, was my oversized red ice chest in the middle of the floor. Even more surprising, it was still banded shut. With my claim check in hand, I searched for an attendant to authorize me and my luggage to continue on our way. I could find no one. So without anyone bothering to stop me or to check my baggage, I walked out of the airport and straight to my car.

A year after my return, I tried to contact Hartwig in hopes of planning another trip back to Namibia. Unfortunately, the museum informed me that he had recently finished his three-year-long research project and had returned to Austria to teach at the university and raise his family.

CHAPTER 5

Peru

A Herper in a Birder's Nest

WHEN I RECEIVED A CALL from my friend Angelo Capparella at Louisiana State University (LSU) asking that I assist him on a survey deep in the remote jungles of Peru, I thought he must have been joking. LSU has a phenomenal herpetology department, and I could not understand why they wanted *me* to participate instead of someone from their staff. Angelo's explanation was simple—they could not spare anyone from their herpetology section for nearly three months. Well, there was no way I could leave my work for that long either.

"No problem," Angelo said, "you can join us for as long as you can spare." At the end of the phone call, I put in a request for a month off from work sometime in mid-June of that year (1987).

I had met Angelo nearly ten years earlier at the Carnegie Museum of Natural History in Pittsburgh, Pennsylvania, where he worked as a "bird preparator" (one who makes study skins and skeletal mounts from bird carcasses) and I had been a lab assistant in the herpetology department. Several years thereafter, it had been my good fortune to work with Angelo on an endangered salamander project for the Raleigh State Museum in North Carolina.

Despite his youth at the time (he was then in his late twenties), Angelo had a great deal of experience in ornithology. In fact, he received his Ph.D.

literally days before the Peru trip was to begin. What I did not understand was why an ornithologist was inviting a herpetologist to conduct a reptile and amphibian survey in an unexplored region of Peru. It turned out that this trip was a continuation of an ongoing research project LSU had started almost twenty years earlier. The trip was specifically designed to document the avifauna in an unexplored area of central-eastern Peru, with the hope of discovering new bird species. Since I was the only herpetologist among a dozen other scientists and researchers on the expedition, my work represented only a small fraction of the group's efforts. Although most of the other "players" on the trip were ornithologists, the group also included botanists, entomologists, a medical doctor, and even a book author. Although Angelo was the organizer of the expedition, he was not the trip leader. That distinction went to John O'Neill, another team member with an even more impressive resume in the field of ornithology. O'Neill is a world-renowned bird artist whose artwork has been published in numerous field guides, journals, magazines, and natural history books. He also has described several new species of birds and has had the honor of having several bird species named after him. John is without doubt one of the leading authorities on Neotropical ornithology.

Another notable team member, Al Gentry, was considered one of the world's great botanists. As a world traveler, he had done more botanical research and field collecting than could possibly have been listed in these pages. Unfortunately, a devastating airplane accident in 1993 took his life and that of another notable scientist, ornithologist Ted Parker. (Ted was also scheduled to be on our expedition but was unable to catch up to us due to other work-related obligations.) With the passing of these two men, the scientific community suffered an incalculable loss. Among Ted's many accomplishments was his ability to identify birds solely by their calls. This talent was so well developed that he could recognize a new species of bird just by its call, without first having seen the bird itself.

Despite the team's twenty years of research experience in Peru, an expedition of this magnitude was an incredibly complicated undertaking. In addition to contacting all the members of the team to coordinate their simultaneous departures (mind you, this was from at least half a dozen different states), the leaders had to assemble all supplies (this itself was a monumental task, as we had more than a ton and a half of equipment); obtain the necessary collecting permits in Peru; hire native guides; book local accommodations beforehand; acquire boats to haul our goods and people; and complete many other tasks that would overwhelm even the most seasoned traveler.

••

All members of the team met in the small village of Pucallpa in central-eastern Peru—not much more than an enlarged dot on the map. The plan was to stock up on local foods and other provisions and then hire a boat to ferry us to an even more remote village that would allow us access to smaller river tributaries. These tributaries, in turn, would eventually lead to our final destination, a base camp only a few miles from the Brazilian border off the Rio Shesha. In reality, however, plans that seem well thought-out in advance often become little more than wishful fantasies. This axiom should be familiar to any experienced traveler, and it was one with which we would all soon become reacquainted.

When the last of the expedition members finally arrived at the Gran Hotel Mercedes, we convened in the restaurant for a well-deserved, hearty meal, giving us the opportunity to meet one another and discuss plans for our upcoming adventure. The scene seemed surreal: twelve of us sitting around a large table, with O'Neill at the head, spouting chapter and verse regarding our imminent future. There was something almost biblical about this gathering.

Aside from bird specialists, we were fortunate to have those with additional expertise, such as Tony Meyer, join our ranks. He was not only an accomplished ornithologist but also a medical doctor. John was skilled at putting together a well-rounded team of experts who each, like Tony, displayed more than one talent. Sitting across the table from me was another non-ornithologist, Don Stap. He was an author, and this was his third year to accompany LSU members specifically to write a book on ornithological field research. (Three years after the trip, Don published his book: *A Parrot without a Name: The Search for the Last Unknown Birds on Earth*.) Sitting near me at the dining room table was Donna Schmidt, a young scientist from New Mexico, one of the most skilled bird preparators around. As we chatted and dined, Donna suddenly stopped chewing and held her lower jaw in apparent discomfort.

"I just bit a piece of metal, and I think I cracked a tooth," she lamented as she spit out a mouthful of rice. Opening her mouth, she leaned toward John and asked him to examine her teeth. Sure enough, her tooth was shattered. Despite her protest that repairing the broken molar would delay our departure, we decided that Donna needed immediate attention and would return to Lima with John the next morning. We estimated that this would cost us only one extra day; the rest of the team would proceed with our scheduled departure two days later. John was confident he could catch up with us by late afternoon on the second day, if not sooner.

• •

At the crack of dawn, we were ready to go to the marketplace to stock up on provisions. Since there would be no other place along the way to buy basics such as bulk foods and certain other materials, this would be our last chance to obtain supplies. The sights, sounds, and smells of the marketplace were an assault on the senses. The crowded streets were packed with vendors of every type, their rickety stalls lining alleyways from one end of town to the other. Every conceivable food product could be found in this makeshift shantytown. Many tables held uncovered meats and foods of unknown varieties, all equally infested with countless flies and other insects. One entire section of the market was devoted exclusively to fish. Entrance to this area was at one's own risk, because the stench of rotten fish and garbage was more than most could endure. Even though many stalls had fresh and even live fish, the sheer volume of all that "food" crammed into this closed environment was just too much to stomach.

Sitting atop every electric pole, streetlight, and building were countless black vultures, drawn there by the overpowering odor of decaying flesh. Adding to the smell was the tremendous volume of garbage piled several feet high throughout the entire marketplace, where all manner of disgusting refuse was discarded. Other vendors were selling live birds, monkeys, turtles, pigs, and any other animal they could find. Several booths sold only animal parts, such as those of turtles or pigs. Here one could purchase just the legs or heads of these once-tortured animals.

With several hours remaining before we returned to our hotel, Don announced that he would like to track down the fossil of an animal that supposedly once resided here in Pucallpa. After he shared this bit of information with Tony, the two of them set out to locate what was supposed to be the fragment of a giant species of crocodilian. Having been gone most of the day, they finally returned to inform me that their mission was successful. After numerous false leads, they had found the location of the mysterious fossil—a doctor's office.

The three of us hailed a taxi and within minutes were waiting outside the office. While Tony went inside to negotiate a chance to view this ancient treasure, Don mentioned to me that he had read about this fossil in

Busy street scene in Pucallpa, eastern Peru. Note black vultures perched on rooftops and electric poles waiting to feed on garbage and food scraps.

Peter Matthiessen's book, *The Cloud Forest,* which was written in 1960. When Tony finally emerged, he instructed us to follow him back to a dark and dingy room.

There, in a corner of the doctor's office, was a large wooden crate. Judging from the thick layer of dust covering the lid, we assumed it had not been opened in years. After a few minutes, the doctor proudly explained to us (in Spanish) that this was a rare national treasure that the people of Pucallpa were proud to have in their possession. I seriously doubted that any of the locals had seen the fossil, for it appeared to have remained undisturbed in this room for years. Eventually someone produced a crowbar and with considerable effort (no doubt due to the weight of all the dust) opened the crate. Inside was a rather large portion of the upper jaw of what appeared to be a giant crocodile. It was all that remained of the extinct animal. The tooth sockets, all empty, were of considerable size, probably twice the diameter of my thumb. We all stared at the object and tried to imagine what a thirty-five-foot-long crocodilian might have looked like in the rivers and swamps of this remote region.

I took several photographs of the fossil and wondered why such a significant find was not in a museum where it could be studied and made accessible to the public. I was later informed that a lot of controversy surrounds the jaw and that at least half a dozen people claim to be its rightful owner. While we stared, mesmerized by the fossil, we could hear loud coughing coming from the room next door. Tony, a physician by profession, wandered into the adjoining room and noticed an X-ray film hanging from a light box. He asked the doctor if that was in fact the X-ray from the young lady sitting in the examining room. When the doctor said

Fossilized portion of the upper jaw of a giant crocodile housed in a doctor's office in a remote part of Pucallpa, eastern Peru.

yes, Tony abruptly suggested that we leave immediately. The X-ray revealed that the woman had an advanced case of tuberculosis, and Tony urged us to vacate the building as soon as possible.

By late afternoon, the group had purchased all of its supplies. Unfortunately, this would substantially increase the weight of our gear, which at times would have to be hand-carried. Our luggage now included thirty-two oversized footlockers (a total of more than four thousand pounds), not to mention all of our personal backpacks, camera bags, suitcases, and the like.

• •

The following morning's departure was hectic. First we had to remove all the equipment stored in the dining area. This was no easy task as we had over two tons of material. Even with all of our team members nearby and watching, one of Don's bags was snatched from under our noses. Before we realized it, the thief and the bag were gone. Fortunately, none of the stolen items was irreplaceable: some clothing, a few books, and some medications, but not much else. Now we had to tighten security over our belongings as we faced the laborious task of getting everything from the hotel to the river, over a mile away. Since our "confirmed" truck driver failed to show up as promised, the ordeal became even more complicated, but eventually we rented a large, dilapidated truck to ferry all our baggage to the riverfront. Of special concern was the fact that John was not going to accompany us upriver as he had to take Donna to a dentist in Lima. He did not believe that Donna would get appropriate treatment here in Pucallpa, where many dentists still used drills powered by a treadle. From now on, Angelo was in charge.

The scene at the river was nearly as revolting as that in the market-place. Most notable were the endless piles of garbage strewn everywhere. Amidst the stinking trash were numerous severely emaciated dogs scavenging any scrap of "edible" food they could find. Here, too, were hundreds of vultures fighting each other for pieces of rotten fish and other sundry debris that littered every square foot of the shoreline. In the water were hundreds of boats, large and small, some of which seemed incapable of staying afloat. Most of these were tied to another boat or to a sturdy pole to keep them from sinking.

With every team member working feverishly, we eventually loaded all our belongings onto a giant boat known locally as a *colectivo* (essentially, the equivalent of a bus on water). The boat appeared to be "seaworthy," but personal space was sorely lacking. In addition to our crew and their luggage, many locals were also traveling upriver. This made for a cramped ride, as there was no room to put even our feet on the floor. At our launch site, the Ucayali River was vast and fast-moving, but we knew that the farther upriver we traveled, the smaller the river would become and the more difficult navigating would be.

Our first destination was the small village of Abujao (A-bu-how). We were told the journey would take about five or six hours, but we quickly learned that timetables in the tropics are merely illusions. The *colectivo* stopped at numerous small villages along the way, dropping off and picking up passengers at each tiny settlement. Occasionally, as the water level dropped, giant piranhas, many of them seven inches long, jumped into the boat. Despite their large size, enormous teeth (nearly half an inch in length), and aggressive reputation (though mostly undeserved), most of the locals on the boat never even flinched when one of these fish landed

View of Ucayali River in Pucallpa showing the variety of boats available for hire. Notice the black vultures feeding on garbage at the water's edge.

at their feet. On the other hand, our team members oohed and aahed when they observed firsthand these fascinating and legendary fish.

By sunset we still had not arrived at our destination. As darkness fell, we resorted to handheld flashlights to illuminate our way along the rest of the journey through the murky waters. When we finally reached Abujao, it was completely dark. After eight hours of being cooped up in extremely uncomfortable positions, we now had the monumental task of unloading two tons of equipment in the dark and moving it up a steep, slippery embankment. As we began the backbreaking work, the locals selected viewing positions along the ridge overlooking their village. From here they watched with glee and laughed as we struggled for several hours to secure our belongings in a makeshift hut that doubled as the local bar. Eventually, several locals assisted us, and we were soon settled in for the night. Except for a small, unfinished building that served as a makeshift "hospital," there were few accommodations. While there was room for most of the team in this structure, several members chose to spend the night among our stacks of luggage piled on the "barroom" floor. I felt sorry for them, as the mosquitoes at this place were among the worst I had ever experienced. It was late, and after a few warm Cokes, orange Fantas, and locally brewed beers, most of us called it a night.

• •

We were up early the next morning and anxious to begin our long journey up the Rio Shesha. Our Peruvian guide, Manuel Sanchez, who had been part of the LSU expeditions since they began in 1967, was perhaps the most valuable member of the team. His intimate knowledge of the rivers, his expertise with regard to the local wildlife, his skill as an outdoorsman, and his ability to communicate with various indigenous peoples made him an invaluable partner. His first task was to get enough small boats to carry the team and all the equipment upriver to our final destination some forty miles (sixty-five kilometers) away. Although this seemed like only a short distance from our present location, it would take several days to reach the main campsite because of the rapidly receding waters of the Rio Shesha. While we waited for some word about our boats, we took advantage of the delay to reorganize all the large footlockers. We had thirty-two of them, as well as a dozen *costales* (a kind of large fiber-reinforced bag used throughout Peru), each one full of equipment and supplies that had to be removed and inventoried, one piece at a time. By late afternoon, Angelo and Tony finally found the one footlocker I most wanted to see. It weighed nearly fifty pounds and was full of chocolate. (Good old number seventeen, a locker I kept in sight at all times.)

By now it was getting dark, and we still had no boats at our disposal. I passed the time wandering through the woods in search of herpetofauna. Due to the time of year (June—the dry season), not much was moving in the nearby jungle. I managed to find a few anoles and a couple of common frogs but nothing substantial. I photographed them and released them back to the wild.

When Manuel finally returned with word about the rented boats, he informed us that he had hired two small dugouts, and that we should plan to leave early the next morning. Looking at our large volume of luggage, we knew there was no way just two boats could carry it all upriver. However, Manuel expressed confidence that he would be able to secure another boat in the morning. The plan at this point was that the boats would transport our equipment, and we (the dozen team members) would walk until additional boats could pick us up en route.

In the brief time we had been in Peru, I had seen our plans change almost by the hour. Such is the nature of these expeditions.

Just after sunset, Manuel began the evening meal. Usually, meals consisted of some kind of pasta or rice; if we were lucky, tuna or other protein would be included as well. Due to the constantly changing schedule and the numerous tasks that all the members routinely performed, we often ate whenever the opportunity arose. I had anticipated this and had brought with me numerous snack bars, hard candy, and other munchies that I stored in various pockets of my already overstuffed camera vest. With nearly thirty pockets to search, I often found it was a chore to locate the appropriate treat, what with film, batteries, collecting gear, rubber bands, insect repellant, and so much more crammed into the jacket as well. The other team members often made fun of me as I looked for a particular item, and Don quipped that I became associated with the sound of Velcro tearing apart.

The following morning we were up early. After breakfast and the arrival of an additional boat, we began the arduous task of transporting our belongings down to the river's edge. What a sight. Most footlockers weighed more than seventy-five pounds, and it took two of us to carry each of these albatrosses down the steep, slippery bank to the waiting boats. The locals, who now gathered en masse to watch as we feebly tried to navigate this impossible course, eventually assisted us by carrying the heavier trunks down the treacherous embankment. Each man shouldered a footlocker and carried it onto the boat by balancing himself along the boat's edge with grace and ease. The outcome of our efforts soon became obvious; there was no way all the items would fit on the three small boats. As we loaded more and more pieces onto the *peki-pekis* (the local name for these vessels, derived from the sound the two-stroke engine belts out as it propels the vessel through the water), we could see that the weight just was too much. Each boat was barely afloat, and two of them were slowly taking on water. After several attempts to rearrange the overloaded boats, we finally came up with the proper balance of equipment that ultimately kept them from sinking.

Al Gentry, the botanist, had not been able to wait to begin our journey upriver. He had very limited time to spend in Peru, most of it ticking away as we awaited our departure. Together with a local guide and an assistant, he had found a small dugout a day before our departure and had begun the laborious process of heading to our final destination. In addition to a few bare necessities, such as food and potable water, Al had taken a chain saw with him, with which he planned to saw through the numerous fallen logs that reportedly had been exposed upstream by the rapidly decreasing water level. With it, he could clear a path for us in advance, thus considerably reducing our travel time.

The plan now changed from waiting around for additional boats to walking along the riverbank until we could be picked up at some point along the way. This meant reducing the weight of our backpacks to the bare minimum, since we had no idea whether we would be walking for ten minutes or ten hours. Fortunately, we walked for just half an hour before being rescued by a sizable *peki-peki*. As we piled into the boat, each of us jockeyed for optimal seating positions. For the best viewing opportunities, everyone wanted to be at the bow, but a pecking order was eventually established, and we were finally on our way.

The river at this point was several hundred feet wide. We knew this was only a temporary luxury and that soon we would be squeezed into smaller and even more precarious tributaries. Without the benefit of cloud cover, we were baking in the midmorning sun. Being extremely sun-sensitive, I covered my head with a pillowcase that I kept tucked under my belt. I am sure that I looked like an escaped mental patient adorned with a bright orange *babushka*. Adding to the discomfort were the small, hard boards that we used as seats. The seats were set far down near the bottom of the boat, making the legroom cramped and extremely uncomfortable. Despite all this, and even though John, Donna, and a third team member had not yet returned from the dentist in Lima, we were glad finally to be on our way.

••

Primitive huts lined the banks of the muddy river: most had palm-thatched roofs, no doors or covered windows, and dirt floors. Small children performed their daily rituals such as washing clothes in the filthy river water, using oversized machetes to clear space for crop planting, tending their pigs and goats, or just swimming and playing in the puddles of their coffee-colored front yards. Chickens and emaciated dogs scampered around the humble dwellings.

Based on the rapidly declining water level, we estimated our travel time to the main campsite to be no more than one or two days. With the sun now setting, we looked for an appropriate place to spend the night, and as we rounded a bend in the river, we found one. Since our boats were quite rickety, we decided they should be emptied of all equipment lest the tremendous weight, combined with the numerous small leaks, would sink them during the night. Before losing daylight altogether, we scrambled to set up makeshift tents while Manuel prepared dinner. Beans and rice were the staple diet for most of the meals, but after a long, rough, exhausting ride, no one was complaining.

Mosquitoes were usually not a problem when the boats were moving, but when we were stuck on a sandbar with no breeze, these insects were brutal. After hastily consuming our meal, we retired to our individual tents, where we were regaled by the loud music played from one of the boatmen's radios. Sleep was nearly impossible.

When I awoke at 6:00 A.M., the garbled and mostly blurred music from the radio was still playing; the guides had already loaded the boats. After a quick cup of coffee or hot chocolate, we were back in the boats, ready for a new day. Now that we were farther upstream, contact with locals had become rare. In an extremely remote area we came across an elderly man in his tiny dugout. He had been fishing and was eager to trade some of his recent catch for whatever supplies we would make available to him, especially batteries, coffee, butter, and, of course, money. We obliged him by giving him what we could spare. As he paddled by, I noticed that he had a container loaded with dozens of eggs wedged between his clothing and a bucket of fish. These were not chicken eggs but those of the yellow-footed tortoise *(Chelonoidis [Geochelone] denticulata)*.

The small tributaries of the Rio Shesha were tapering off to little more than rivulets no wider than a dozen or so feet. The water's depth was also beginning to concern us. At times, with all our combined weight, we scraped the bottom of the tributary in less than a foot of water. Occasionally, it became necessary to get out of the boat and push it over the large tree snags that blocked our way. The closer we came to our final destination, the more obstacles we faced. Although we could see where Al Gentry had recently cut through the logs and fallen tree limbs that bisected the small stream, it did not appear that his handiwork benefited *us* very much. For the remainder of our journey, we proceeded at a snail's pace, stopping every few minutes to extricate our boats from barriers that hindered our progress.

At one particular impasse, Oscar, our second Peruvian guide, jumped from the boat and disappeared into the nearby woods. Initially I thought he was so frustrated by the frequent delays that he had abandoned us and was proceeding on foot to the main campsite. However, he returned a minute later with a large piece of tree bark. But this was no ordinary bark; it was bark from a *setico,* better known as the *Cecropia* tree. The underside of this bark is covered with a thick, viscous slime, and the indigenous people use it for many different purposes. In our case, Oscar placed the bark directly on top of the log blocking our path, with the slimy side facing upward. The rest of us, now standing in knee-deep water, were able to effortlessly drag the boat across the piece of slick bark and over the logjam. This procedure was repeated two more times, freeing the other dugouts as well. After we passed this obstacle, Oscar placed the *setico* bark under his seat for possible reuse in the future. I could not imagine how I would get out of here in three weeks when the water level would be even lower.

With the water level so low and our young guides anxious to return to "civilization" to spend their soon-to-be-earned money, they began to navigate the shallow waters with reckless abandon. They raced with each other, repeatedly forgetting about the submerged logs that mined the river. Collisions with these logs at full speed capsized the boats several times, thus dumping our belongings into the muddy river. Without a fluent command of the language, none of us felt comfortable enough to chastise these youths, fearing they might retaliate by unloading all of our possessions on the nearest sandbar and forcing us to walk the rest of the way. The situation eventually got worse, and Manuel finally approached the boatmen and scolded them for their irresponsible behavior.

By now, I had become extremely restless, what with the constant sunshine and heat scorching me to a crisp, the frustration of being unable to do any herping despite the endless expanse of jungle that surrounded me, and my cramped body position in the boat. The ornithologists, on the other hand, seemed too preoccupied with the endless variety of birds that perched in the adjacent woods or flew nearby to concern themselves with such minor inconveniences. I envied them. I did manage to observe some birds (without the benefit of binoculars, which each birder had permanently attached around his or her neck). I spent much of my time pointing my 500-mm camera lens at any animal I could see in a futile attempt to photograph it. Between the constant motion and vibration of the boat and the incessant movement of the birds, I really did not have much hope that any of the photos would turn out well. Nonetheless, many of the birds were exquisite and entertaining to watch.

Peru has more than seventeen hundred bird species. In this remote region alone, more than four hundred species can be found, nearly half the total number of species inhabiting the entire United States. Here, enormous raptors commonly perched on barren tree trunks; colorful parrots of all sizes flew above, chattering noisily; giant kingfishers skimmed the water in search of fish; hummingbirds adorned nearly every flowering plant along the banks; and spectacular sunbitterns *(Eurypyga helias)*, whose wings resemble the intricate paintings of Old World masters, escorted us from sandbar to sandbar.

• •

After two days on the water, we finally caught sight of Al Gentry's boatman coming toward us from upriver. He handed us a note from Al, stating that he would try to remove as many river obstacles as he could, but that he had loaned the chain saw to some locals who also needed it for river travel. This was disturbing, for we had already encountered several logjams from which we could barely extricate ourselves. We, in turn, handed the lead boatman a note to pass on to O'Neill in which we stated that we would likely be at the main campsite a day late and that we hoped he would catch up to us soon.

Occasionally our boat passed close to a small bush near shore, or even one in the middle of the river, where a snake was basking in the sun's warming rays. Most times we sailed rapidly by the reptiles, for I was unable to coerce the boatmen to slow down or stop. I was convinced they pretended not to hear my pleas, not due to time constraints, but rather because they were afraid I would try to capture the snakes and put them at risk of snakebite. (All the snakes we saw en route were nonvenomous.) The ornithologists suffered a similar fate when Tony saw what he thought was a harpy eagle *(Harpia harpyja)*. He was much more vocal than I and, upon seeing the bird, screamed loudly for our boatman to stop. Again the boatman ignored the request and continued on, focusing on the shallow waters ahead. Disturbed by our loud engines, the bird quickly flew off, apparently with something in its talons. Tony was furious.

Although most of the barriers in our way were small logs or an occasional entanglement of vines, some obstacles were truly enormous. Al had cut through most of them, but due to the extremely low water level, a few of them stopped us in our tracks. At one of these giant tree falls, we were forced to unload some of our belongings and pass them over the tree. In addition, some of the team members either had to lie flat in the bottom of the boat or, to avoid being injured by the massive trees, get out and climb over the obstacle. As we approached one tree, we startled a group of bats (probably pencil-nosed bats) that were clinging to the underside of the bark awaiting nightfall to begin their search for flying insects. When we glided under it, the boat scraped against the trunk, tearing loose a piece of bark and causing it to drop in the water next to me. Immediately, a small gecko *(Gonatodes* sp.) swam toward shore, but I grabbed it before it escaped. At last, a reptile. (I coined a new phrase at this point: mercy herping.)

• •

By the middle of the third day, we finally reached our destination and began the laborious task of unloading the boats. Due to the reckless behavior of our boatmen, nearly all of our belongings—most of which were now soaked—needed to be placed in the sun to dry. One footlocker contained nothing but hundreds of batteries, and it took several of us the entire day to wipe off each one before setting it out to dry. In addition, all our clothing, tents, books, collecting equipment, food, and even ammunition had to be removed from the waterlogged luggage and hung out to dry. We also spread out into the woods to search for places to set up our tents, never wandering far lest we should become isolated from the safety and sanctuary of the main compound. We were not as concerned about meeting gangs of unfriendly natives as we were about encountering dangerous wildlife or becoming lost in this vast, unexplored region.

A four-foot-long
blunt-headed tree
snake *(Imantodes
cenchoa)* hangs from
a thin branch high
off the ground. Its
large eyes and
elliptical pupils help
it locate frogs and
lizards at night.

Manuel, Oscar, and several other guides began the time-consuming task
of setting up the structures that over the next two months would be our
dining hall; main animal research facility; equipment storage building; and
yes, even "toilets," which were nothing more than deep holes in the ground,
each with a sturdy stick next to the opening for the user to hold onto so as
not to fall in. Amazingly, these "modern conveniences" were made solely
with local plant material. These men were truly master carpenters. With
just a machete, they assembled structures that most handymen back home
could build only with all the modern electrical devices at their disposal.

By early evening, we had completed most of the chores. I still had time
before dinner to investigate the areas around camp for reptiles and am-

phibians. Whoever had chosen this site had known what he was doing. Bordered by a small tributary of the Rio Shesha on the west, we were surrounded on all other sides by virgin rain forest. Although the river here was shallow and muddy, we used it to bathe in, wash our clothes in, and even drink from. We not only boiled the water for drinking and cooking, but we also purified it with iodine tablets and a filter.

Before dark, I found a large toad by the water's edge. It was robust with dark red spots scattered on its posterior half. The spots stood out in stark contrast to the amphibian's overall pale brown coloration. When I picked it up, it exuded a thick, yellow substance from its large parotoid glands (oval structures located behind the eyes of most toads, from which toxins are produced). This kind of chemical warfare is typical of a toad's defense behavior. Had I touched my eyes or mouth after handling the toad, I would have suffered painfully swollen eyes or possibly have frothed at the mouth. Although I had not seen this species firsthand before, I recognized it as a smooth-fronted toad *(Bufo guttatus)*. My first catch at the new camp proved significant, as it was the only example of its kind I would find during my entire stay.

As usual, dinner was expertly prepared and consisted of pasta, beans, and tuna fish. After wolfing down my food, I left camp in search of nocturnal creatures. In less than five minutes, I saw a beautifully patterned blunt-headed tree snake *(Imantodes cenchoa)* resting on a tree limb about seven feet above my head. I leaped into the air and, to my surprise, managed to grab the snake from the twig on which it was crawling. This is a gentle and inoffensive species, and despite my rough interruption of its search for food, it made no threatening or aggressive moves toward me. The snake exists throughout much of Latin America: I have found it in every tropical American country I have visited. I never tire of seeing it. Nearly five feet long, pencil-thin, and with oversized, bulging eyes, this is an amazing creature to watch as it creeps precariously from a tiny wisp of a branch on one tree to an even smaller branch on another, almost one body length away. In my excitement to capture the snake, I let out a scream that brought most of the camp to my aid. With profuse apologies, I assured them I had not been bitten or consumed by some wild predator but had merely been overly enthusiastic about catching the first snake of the trip. Although snakes in the tropics are diverse, they are generally very secretive, and sometimes it takes days to find one in the dense tropical vegetation.

The advantage of looking for reptiles and amphibians at night with a flashlight is that instead of being distracted by the sights and sounds of everything around you, you simply focus your attention on the narrow beam of light in front of you. Thus, you can detect the slightest movement of even the smallest animal. This method of collecting is my favorite, as I can lose myself in the moment and tune out everything around me except the flashlight in my hand and the animal caught in its beam.

• •

My sleep was intermittent because I thought it was raining in the early morning hours when in fact it was just the constant dripping of condensation in the jungle around my tent.

At 6:00 A.M., when I finally stumbled out of my tent, I could see that I was the last one awake, not because I had slept late, but because nearly all the other team members were ornithologists who are ready to search for birds as early as 4:30 A.M. Pete, one of LSU's newest graduates on his first trip to the tropics (and by his own admission the "camp slave"), handed me a small plastic bag containing a lizard he had caught early that morning.

"Cool gecko, don't you think, Paul?" he asked in the exuberant voice of someone who has been up for several hours.

"Thanks, Pete, but it's an anole, not a gecko," I replied. But my comment went unnoticed as Pete quickly walked to the breakfast table where Manuel had prepared a sumptuous meal of pancakes, jelly, and hot chocolate. Not being one to pass up hot chocolate, I staggered over to the kitchen table where I was treated to some of the most delicious hot cakes I had ever eaten. Despite the lack of good old Log Cabin syrup, I eagerly devoured three pancakes then washed them down with two cups of steaming hot chocolate. Even though we were in the tropics, mornings tended to be rather cool, and hot drinks were as cherished as the rarest catch of the day.

On this trip, the culinary experiences in camp were nothing short of extraordinary. Nightly, the guides showed up with a different rain forest creature for the stew pot, ranging from diminutive tortoises and giant birds to monkeys and deer. Not all of us shared in these exotic nightly banquets. Some declined the offerings because the taste was poor, while others thought some of the dishes were simply in poor taste. One night a guide brought a yellow-footed tortoise into camp as the intended main dish. Although I was immediately repulsed by the thought of eating such a magnificent beast, I was intrigued by the way in which the guide transported it. He had wrapped a sturdy vine precisely between the carapace and plastron, thereby covering the tortoise's head, legs, and tail. This

Peruvian guide carrying the "turtle purse" (yellow-footed tortoise) back to camp to be used as the evening meal.

prevented the animal from struggling and exposing its limbs and head, which could possibly injure the handler. The end result was a kind of "turtle purse" that he wore like a shoulder bag. With the idea of releasing it later, I asked if I could purchase the animal, but the owner refused, and ever so reluctantly, I accepted the tortoise's fate. Needless to say, I skipped dinner.

On the day a curassow was brought to camp, I beheld a sight that was reminiscent of a flock of vultures descending on a recent kill. The ornithologists wanted the skin and bones for research, the cooks wanted the meat for dinner, and the photographers clamored for prized photos. The bird was a razor-billed curassow *(Mitu tomentosa),* a species not commonly seen. Due to the chef's eagerness to prepare dinner, the bird's feathers were plucked almost immediately, rendering the skin useless as a research specimen. In the end, the skeleton was saved, the chef prepared dinner, and the photographers got nothing (except a good meal).

The same guide who captured the curassow returned another night with additional game. This time, it was an adult red howler monkey (*Alouatta seniculus*) he had recently shot. He removed the dead female from his shoulder bag then reached in and pulled out her infant which was wounded but still alive. This sight upset everyone in camp (the "gringos" anyway), and even Tony, who admits he is no Bambi lover, was visibly distraught. I do not know if everyone's negative reaction influenced the chef, but the dead monkey was not prepared for dinner. Instead it was left out all night with the crying baby clinging to it. At the break of dawn, the muffled cries of the baby could still be heard as it searched for comfort from its lifeless mother. As we began milling about the camp, we each had to face the issue again. Sensing our distaste over this situation, Oscar finally took both monkeys down to the river and drowned the infant. As we lamented the morning's events, we were mindful that we were merely guests in this country and could not insert our values and ways of thinking into the natives' customs and beliefs. We were bound to silence by social and political protocols in our host country, and we had to defer control over these types of situations to the local guides.

For me, the issue of a dead animal carcass was not the source of the controversy: watching an animal's prolonged and needless suffering was. As I reflect on the sadness I felt at the time, I now realize that the sorrow has actually grown as my travels and life experiences have awakened in me a greater appreciation for *all* animals.

••

That morning, Angelo, Manuel, and Gabriel (a student from the university in Lima) were cutting a path from our campsite to a group of nearby mountains that were intended to be our final destination. O'Neill's original plan was to set up camp in these isolated mountains, which he believed might hold some new and undescribed bird species. The team came back three hours later, however, only to report that despite their progress, the mountains were still four or five hours away if we walked briskly. With so much equipment to carry, this was not feasible. We made the decision to stay in our present camp; however, if some among the group chose to do so, they could make a temporary campsite near the distant mountains. From these campsites, individuals could make short exploratory forays to the mountains to possibly reveal what bird species occur there.

Since we knew nothing about the whereabouts of John, Donna, and Marta (Manuel's wife, the camp cook), we were all apprehensive about the future of the expedition. It had been nearly a week since we said good-bye to them, and we had expected only a one- or two-day delay.

Another issue on everyone's mind, although few spoke of it, was the disappearance of our botanist, Al Gentry. We knew he had arrived at our camp several days before us, because Angelo found the liquid nitrogen bottles Al had hidden here. (These large metal containers are standard equipment for researchers venturing into remote regions where there is no electricity and where animal tissues must be stored at very cold temperatures (below −40 degrees Farenheit).) Yet, several days had elapsed since our last contact with him.

Early on the third morning in camp, as breakfast was being served, we heard voices from across the river. There, to our amazement, in the thick tangle of underbrush, were Al and his guide, tearing their way by hand through the dense vegetation. Al appeared haggard and completely exhausted, and the guide, Camilo, looked nearly dead. It turned out they had lost their way in the jungle days ago and had survived by eating nuts, a palm heart, and snails. Because they had had no food, water, compass, matches, or even a machete, it is to their credit that they were able to survive at all. While Al explained the events of the last couple of days, he gulped down two cups of hot chocolate while alternately devouring several pancakes. He now had only two days remaining in Peru, so within minutes of completing his meal, he grabbed some equipment, looked around at the gathered masses, and explained that he was going back into the field again. Whether or not he was serious, I really did not know, but he did ask, "Does anyone want to go with me?" There were no takers.

I remained close to camp and spent nearly every waking moment searching for reptiles and amphibians. I had good success catching several species of frogs, a few anoles, and a lizard that I initially thought was a common ameiva. Surprisingly, it turned out to be something entirely different, though closely related: *Kentropyx altamazonica*, a kind of "keeled-bellied" ameiva. Unlike ameivas, which have smooth ventral scales, these lizards have a pronounced ridge or keel on each belly scale.

By now, the birders had set up their mist nets at strategic locations in and around the main campsite. Other nets were located a considerable distance away in an effort to capture species that might be disturbed by our activities.

Setting up mist nets takes time. First, the ornithologists have to find an ideal location. Then they must clear the area of tree limbs and undergrowth to prevent the foliage from becoming tangled in the net. Next, they pound sturdy poles or trees into the earth at either end of the net to secure it and hold it taut. Finally, the net itself, which may be over thirty feet long and ten feet high, has to be firmly secured to the frame, so the net will not fall apart or come loose when birds are ultimately removed from it. This is extremely hard work, and each researcher takes it very seriously. By day's end, there were over a dozen nets in place. All that was left now was to wait for the birds.

Inspired by all the activity around me, I began to set up my own traps. Unlike the sophisticated and efficient mist nets, the "sky canopy trap" and "funnel traps" I brought to catch reptiles and amphibians were primitive. Just before my departure from the United States, I had read in a herpetological journal about a researcher who used a series of small minnow traps connected to a long piece of netlike material suspended high in the canopy to catch frogs, lizards, and snakes. His setup had yielded surprising results—he had caught numerous small reptiles and amphibians. I had hoped to use this device to discover what herps existed around camp at elevations fifty to seventy-five feet above the forest floor.

Setting up this monstrosity was grueling. First, I had to find a way to get high up in the treetops. I had purchased some climbing gear to bring on this trip, but I was not proficient in its use. The first thing I needed was a rock or other such object to tie to the end of my climbing rope so that I might hurl it into the canopy where it would, with luck, wrap around or catch on a sturdy branch. The task was difficult, as there were no rocks in the area. Improvising, I "borrowed" the camp's hammer and used it to set up my ascending rope. Because the hammer was an important camp tool, most of the team members were a little perturbed with me for repeatedly getting it stuck in the trees, then soliciting the assistance of the guides to remove it. After several unsuccessful attempts, I finally managed to climb the tree and set the trap. Much to my disappointment, all that it caught were a few grasshoppers and a handful of leaves. Considering the effort I put into this project, it was not worth the trouble.

A bit more successful was the "funnel trap," which is nothing more than a plastic container sunk into the ground with a piece of smooth funnel-shaped metal or plastic over the opening. If a small creature, such as a lizard, snake, or even small mammal, steps on the funnel, the animal slides through the opening and is trapped in the container below. To increase the chance of catching something in these traps, a sheet of plastic or similar material is stretched upright between the funnel traps (often twenty-five to fifty feet apart). This increases the odds that the animal will be guided along the "wall" of plastic and fall into the bucket. I had limited success with this trap, catching only a few small lizards and a toad.

• •

On previous trips, I had had to photograph birds held in the hand, and my pictures had included only the head and neck of my subjects. With the possibility of photographing a large variety of birds on this expedition, I brought along a miniature tent that I had made before leaving the States. Simple in design, it resembled a shelter made for a small dog. It was cylindrical, the back wall was made of blue material (to give the appearance of the sky), the sides were white, and the opening consisted of two pieces of cloth held together by strips of Velcro. In its center I placed a small, unobtrusive branch on which I hoped a bird would perch.

Because it had never been tested and since there was a good possibility that once a bird was placed inside it could easily escape, I initially thought I would not be allowed to use it. It did not take long for the mist nets to yield large numbers of captured birds. Not wanting to risk an escape, I waited until a common species had been caught. I then meekly asked if I could try out my "bird photography tent," and to my surprise, permission was granted. Carefully holding the bird, I slipped it into the enclosure through the entrance where the Velcro held the two cloth panels shut.

Bird photography tent used by the author in eastern-central Peru to photograph birds in a more "naturalistic" manner.

When I was sure the bird was well inside the tent, I opened my hand and it immediately flew to and perched on the small branch. I was still nervous but at the same time elated. So far everything was working perfectly. The bird sat calmly on the perch as I set up my tripod-mounted camera and poked the lens through a small opening in the Velcro closure. I thus took several pictures of the entire bird, and to my amazement, it sat still throughout the photo session. It worked. I was thrilled. I still had one risky task ahead of me: removing the bird without letting it escape. To my surprise and delight, I captured the bird with little effort and with no injuries to either the bird or to myself.

More birds followed, including some rare species, and each time the results were the same. Only a single bird escaped, and none was ever injured. Finally I was able to photograph some rare and beautiful birds without having a distracting human hand in the picture.

••

After a night of heavy rain, I knew the next day would bring out some interesting animals. That night, I inhaled my dinner and then immediately sought the sanctity of the surrounding jungle. I had not even left camp, and already I had collected four different species of frogs. One species was one of the largest members of the poison frog family (Dendrobatidae). About two inches in length, the three-striped poison frog, *Epipedobates [Dendrobates] trivittatus,* is exquisite. Mostly black, with three yellow or lime green stripes running down the length of its body, it also has green limbs infused with powder blue splotches.

Due to the heavy rains of the previous evening, that night's theme was definitely "amphibians galore." Most of the frogs I collected during the night belonged to a genus with the greatest diversity in the entire vertebrate world: *Eleutherodactylus,* colloquially referred to as "rain frogs." It is a daunting task to properly identify many of the 650 or so species this genus contains. At our campsite alone, we saw more than two dozen species. Although the majority of these frogs are not very colorful, they have an unusual reproductive cycle. Unlike most anurans, which lay their eggs in water then undergo a metamorphosis from an aquatic tadpole to a juvenile, members of this group completely bypass the tadpole stage. Instead, females lay relatively small numbers of clear, pea-sized gelatinous eggs on land, placing them under leaves, logs, or other surface shelter. When they emerge from the eggs, the completely self-sufficient frogs are tiny replicas of their parents.

A palm salamander
(*Bolitoglossa
peruviana*), a rare
find in the remote
jungle of eastern
Peru.

I knew this would be a productive night for herps, but when my flashlight beam revealed a palm salamander *(Bolitoglossa peruviana)* crawling slowly across a leaf, I was nearly dumbfounded. There are only two known species of salamanders this far south in the tropics, and I thought both of them were rare and seldom seen. I later confirmed this belief when I returned to the States and spoke to the leading authority on New World salamanders, Dr. David Wake. He informed me that, to date, only one or two salamanders have been collected in Peru and that my collection of twelve specimens (the total I saw during my stay) was highly significant. At this point, I could only hope that John would manage to get export permits not only for birds but for herps as well. This would guarantee that preserved specimens would be deposited in a recognized scientific institution where they would be available for study to researchers everywhere.

As I continued to use my flashlight to illuminate the endless wall of jungle foliage and search for signs of life, the beam of light suddenly revealed an unusual emerald green lizard sleeping about five feet above the forest floor with only its hands and feet visible. Although it was a member of the iguana family, this was no common iguana. Referred to as a "dwarf" iguana *(Enyalioides laticeps festae),* since it seldom exceeds two feet in length, this lizard had small, pointed spines all over its tail, back, neck, and even above its eyes. It looked like a miniature dinosaur.

Tonight's foray into the woods lasted into the wee hours of the morning, and by the time I returned to camp, everyone was asleep. This was unusual, since the birders were almost always working on something, even at one or two in the morning. Exhausted from the outing, I was asleep before my head hit the pillow.

Three-striped poison frog *(Epipedobates trivittatus)* found near our camp in eastern Peru.

Although it was the dry season, heavy rains occasionally fell, which gave me the opportunity to work on my herpetological parasitology research project with the birders who were preparing their own specimens in the main prep tent. Despite the large size of the main tent (nearly fifteen by twenty feet), there was little room for personnel once the folding tables, chairs, and various shelves were in place. Yet we all managed to accomplish our individual tasks without too much conflict.

It was fascinating to watch the ornithologists prepare the birds into "study skins." The entire process seemed rather ghoulish. A bird is slit open and all of its "innards" removed. Then cotton is stuffed inside the skin to simulate the approximate size of the bird when it was alive. The skull, however, is left inside the head, and pieces of cotton often protrude from the empty eye sockets, giving the bird a decidedly haunting appearance.

View of the work area in the main preparation research tent that was set up by Oscar and Manuel in an unexplored area in Peru's eastern rain forest.

Of great interest to me was the birder's "ledger," a book that lists all the preserved birds in all the museums worldwide including whether they are skeletons, whole preserved mounts (much the way reptiles and amphibians are preserved by injecting them with 10 percent formalin), or just stuffed skins. No such volume exists for herpetological specimens.

On these research trips, sleep is often a luxury. I try to begin my day by 6:00 A.M., but this particular morning I did not arise until nearly 7:00 A.M. By then, everyone had finished breakfast, had been out to set the mist nets, had completed their morning chores (washed up at the river, visited the "bathroom," and so forth), and had maybe even caught up on field notes. My goal this morning was to search some little stream tributaries away from camp for small lizards (microteiids) that are usually associated with them. Because much of the surrounding jungle had not been thinned out, I decided to carry a machete in addition to my trusty snake rake (a four-pronged garden tool I use to flip logs and peel bark, thus reducing the risk of bites and stings from wildlife).

As luck would have it, I found a perfect stream only a mile from camp, where I spotted a small brown lizard at the water's edge. I abruptly stopped in my tracks, slowly assumed a crouching position, and raised my hand as I prepared to slap down on the wary animal. When my hand came down on the lizard, we were both covered with mud. Victorious, I rinsed him off in the slow-flowing muddy water, and to my delight I realized that I was holding a species I had not seen before. It was a semiaquatic microteiid (*Neusticurus ecpleopus*), at that time a member of the family Teiidae. It has since been placed in a newly designated family, the Gymnophthalmidae, which distinguishes the large teiids (Teiidae proper)—the tegus ameivas, caiman lizards, and so forth—from these smaller, closely related forms. About six species of these small lizards occur in this area, and by the trip's end, I had caught three of them. Most live near water, where the slightest disturbance causes them to dive in and either hide in the mud or swim rapidly away. Averaging between two and three inches long, they have distinctly keeled scales on the head and body.

On my way back to camp, I found Manuel working on a mist net. He handed me a bag used to hold birds, saying in Spanish, *culebra* (their word for snake). Actually, Latin Americans have several different words for snake. If the serpent is venomous, they refer to it as *víbora* (viper); they also use the word *serpiente* to denote either venomous or nonvenomous species, although these terms vary throughout Latin America. I opened the bag and peered inside; there was the most beautiful chartreuse green Amazonian vine snake *(Xenoxybelis [Oxybelis] argenteus)* I had ever seen. Its lime green coloration was so vivid it seemed to phosphoresce. Like many colubrid species, vine snakes possess enlarged, grooved teeth in the back of their mouths, down which a mild venom slowly flows, eventually entering the victim to paralyze it. The venom is not dangerous to humans: its effect is more like a mosquito bite or a mild bee sting. Yet some large rear-fanged snakes in southern Africa and Southeast Asia are dangerous to humans.

Before reaching camp, I encountered an unusual lizard wedged in the axil of a small tree. I was surprised to see this animal so close to the ground since this kind of whorl-tailed lizard *(Urocentron azureum guentheri)* is normally found high in the canopy, where it lives in hollowed-out tree trunks and limbs. There it subsists almost entirely on a variety of tree-dwelling ants. Rows of short, hard spines encircle the tail from the base to the tip. This spiny armament can be a formidable weapon, which the reptile uses like a mace, swinging its thorny tail abruptly from side to side when provoked. Since this was a relatively small lizard, five inches in total length, I was not concerned with its tail flailing, but I did receive a nasty bite to a finger from its strong jaws.

Luck was definitely on my side today. Passing several decomposing logs in a clearing, I halfheartedly kicked one over, revealing a small fossorial snake similar to the red coffee snakes I had previously observed in Belize. But I had never seen this one before and had only read about it in scientific journals. It has no readily accepted common name but is known scientifically as *Xenopholis scalaris.* Like most small burrowing snakes, this one remains underground or crawls beneath fallen logs, where it searches for its preferred prey of soft-bodied invertebrates, frogs, and small lizards.

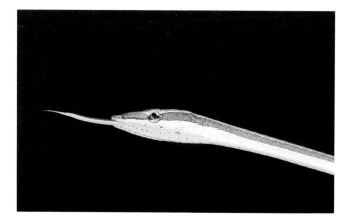

Vine snake *(Xenoxybelis argenteus)* displaying the most vivid chartreuse color seen by the author in any species of snake. Note the snake's distended tongue, which it uses to "smell" its surroundings.

Reaching a maximum size of ten to twelve inches, the snake is red with black blotches scattered along its back.

I returned to camp to photograph my morning's catch and to capture on film whatever birds had been collected. To my surprise and to everyone's delight, John and Donna had finally arrived. While she was in Lima, Donna had had a root canal and received, in addition, a gold crown. Needless to say, this drained her physically as well as financially. John informed us that had we delayed our departure just three more hours, he and Donna would have arrived in time to accompany us. Between the time of our departure and their own late start, however, the water level had gotten so low during the journey that on several occasions they had seriously considered turning back. Nevertheless, they persevered and managed to catch up with us. However, due to the rapidly receding water levels, it had taken them an additional ten days to travel the very same course.

With John finally back in camp, we were all more relaxed. As co-team leader, Angelo had performed his duties admirably and efficiently, but with John's arrival, we expected things to go just a bit more smoothly. His leadership style of allowing people to do their own thing without constant instructions made John a pleasure to work with. After John and Donna were brought up to speed, they were anxious to begin work. John first looked over the birds collected thus far, while Donna immediately settled into the routine of preparing specimens.

A small body of water nearby was home to a colony of hoatzins (*Opisthocomus hoazin*)—truly odd birds. The young have a specialized claw on the outer edge of each wing that enables them to climb back up into the trees after they have launched themselves (in a defensive manner) from the uppermost branches, with any luck landing in the water below.

I had heard about these strange birds years ago and had always wanted to photograph them. Because hoatzins are easily disturbed, we had to steal quietly through the grass, crouching as we approached. Despite these tactics, the birds sensed our presence, and before we could get close enough, the adults took wing. The juveniles all plummeted to earth, taking refuge in the tangles of brush near the edge of the swamp. I lingered a while longer, hoping the hoatzins would eventually return; they did not. While everyone else returned to camp, I stayed behind and continued my search for reptiles and amphibians. Despite my prolonged efforts, I caught only a single anole *(Anolis trachyderma)*. Although not much to look at, it had a distinct orange dewlap, which the males of this species use to attract mates and to ward off other males encroaching on their territories.

Soon after sunset, I found a pair of beautiful snakes on the trunk of an extremely spiny tree. Although they were only a few feet from the ground, I was aware that catching them without injuring myself would be difficult. The spines surrounding them were at least two inches long, and each time I tried to grab one of the reptiles, it sidled up close to the bark of the tree and became irretrievable. Using my long forceps and a small snake hook, I finally extricated the pair. They were snail-eating snakes (*Dipsas catesbyi*), a male and a female, which undoubtedly had recently mated or were about to when they were so rudely interrupted. Their body coloration was light brown with dark brownish black ovals spaced regularly down their backs. Each oval was bordered by a thin white line, making the snakes look more like bars of exotic chocolate than reptiles.

This was a phenomenal night for frogs. After finding half a dozen species I had also collected on previous nights, I found my first smoky jungle frog (*Leptodactylus pentadactylus*). At nearly nine inches in length, this is a true giant and the largest frog in the New World, just slightly larger than our North American bullfrog (*Rana catesbeiana*). When my flashlight beam illuminated the frog, I could see an almost demonic red glow in its large eyes. This is not the normal color of its eyes but rather the luminous reflection from the lining behind the eye, the *tapetum lucidum*. I tried to keep the beam of my flashlight on the frog's eyes, so it could not see me as I approached it. When I was less than five feet from my target, the frog made a 180-degree turn and, with a mighty leap, was out of range.

Later that night, I found several tiny, colorful frogs known as five-striped poison frogs (*Dendrobates quinquevittatus*). Just over half an inch long when fully grown, these amphibians are mostly black with three to five bright yellow stripes running the length of their bodies. Their arms and legs are powder-blue and covered with small black spots bordered by narrow white rings.

I found yet another poison frog species (*Epipedobates [Phyllobates] pictus*), although this one provided something extra: on its back were eight tiny, wriggling tadpoles. In most species of poison frogs, as in this one, the male tends the young. After a female lays her eggs, typically in a bromeliad or other water-filled plant, the male returns periodically to check the plant's water level. If it is too low, the male enters the bromeliad backwards, where he waits for all the tadpoles to climb onto his back. He then descends the tree (sometimes from heights of more than seventy-five feet), finds another bromeliad, backs into it, and allows the tadpoles to claim a new home. Since some tadpole species are egg eaters, the female periodically returns and lays infertile eggs for the growing young to consume.

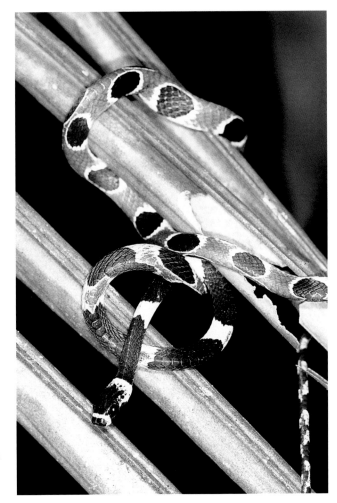

Snail-eating snake
(Dipsas catesbyi) in
eastern Peru whose
coloration reminded
the author of an
exotic chocolate bar.

Rounding out this night was the capture of another representative of the poison frog family—this one, however, was in a different genus *(Colostethus marchesianus)*. The many species of this genus are collectively referred to as "rocket" frogs because of the high, lightning-fast leaps they use to evade predators. They are more somber in coloration than other genera of poison frogs and lack the potent poisons of their more brightly colored relatives.

••

Because I was completely exhausted, tonight's sleep was deeper than usual. The sound of light rain against my tent hastened my slumber, and when I awoke the next morning, rain was still falling. As I staggered out of my tent, I noticed that the river had risen considerably since the previous day, perhaps a foot or more. This was a good sign because it would make the boat trip back the following week much easier. But Oscar, who noisily boated up to our camp, interrupted my thoughts of the future. He informed me that we would return to "civilization" the day after next. The news was rather upsetting since I had planned to stay in the field for almost another week. My only other choice was to return with the rest of the expedition in late August (six weeks away). I gave serious thought to that plan, but it really was not an option; my scheduled vacation time was running out.

With only two days remaining in camp, I now had much to do. Most of all, I wanted at least to visit the mountains that lie on the Brazilian border, our original destination. Don shared this desire, so together we decided to undertake what we thought would be a half-day's journey to the mountain range. Armed with water, food, cameras, bug juice, and rain gear, we promptly left camp. Since we did not know how much time it would take to reach our goal, we decided not to stop along the way to collect specimens or take photographs. By noon, we had found a clearing from which we could get a glimpse of the still-distant mountains. We estimated that to reach them would take another four to five hours, which meant returning to camp in the dark. Given the difficulty of negotiating hills, undergrowth, and slippery streams, we decided to return during daylight. We sat there briefly, looking through binoculars at the cloud-covered peaks, imagining what treasures they might hold. As we rested before starting back, we were both lost in our own silence.

By late afternoon, we had returned to camp—tired, sweaty, and dirty. All I wanted to do was jump in the river and cool off, so I spent the rest of the day cleaning myself in the rising waters of the Shesha River. I am glad I did not think about it at the time, but there is an animal in these watery environs that should give anyone pause while bathing or urinating in them without proper precautions. The animal in question is the *candiru*, better known as the urethra catfish (family Trichomycteridae). This tiny (usually an inch in length, depending on the species), slender, insidious animal homes in on the ammonia scent produced by urine then swims up the urinary tract of the host. Here, armed with a series of spines on its head or back, it locks itself in place so that it cannot be dislodged. In the rare instances when these fish infect humans, they can be removed only by surgery. One can scarcely imagine the agony some animals experience upon such encounters. Unless you don underwear, shorts, or other appropriate protective clothing, my advice is do not urinate in waters where these catfish occur.

Earlier there had been some commotion in the camp, and once I was dry and clothed, I went to see what the excitement was about. In fact, two things were happening. One was the mist-net capture of a rare bird, the crested owl (*Lophostrix cristata*). This was significant, because this species almost never comes down to the forest floor. It is a spectacular bird with exaggeratedly large feathers above each eye, like two huge, bushy eyebrows. I was pleasantly surprised when I received permission to use my bird tent to photograph it. To my delight, the photo setup worked just as well with this large raptor as it did with the many smaller birds that I had photographed earlier.

The other event was even more significant. Several small parrots were heard chattering in a thick bunch of sixty-foot tall bamboo near the edge of the river and at the southern edge of our campsite. Almost since our arrival, nearly everyone in camp had seen and heard the birds, but no one had paid much attention to them. We knew we would be here for some time and that eventually we would get around to investigating them. Well, that time had come. With steady aim, Tony brought down two of the birds. On hearing the rifle blasts so close to camp, everyone scrambled

A crested owl
(*Lophostrix cristata*)
stares blankly at its
captors after being
removed from a mist
net in eastern Peru.

This new species of parrot (*Nannopsittaca dachilleae*) described by John O'Neill was collected during the 1987 expedition to eastern Peru.

out of the main tent to see what the shooting was about. When John was handed one of the birds, he stared at it intently without speaking. He ruffled the wing feathers to check out their pattern and coloration. After a pause, Tony said it looked like a parrotlet (a type of small parrot). O'Neill was mentally going through the numerous species of small parrots, specifically those in the genus *Forpus*, trying to arrive at an identification. I was intrigued. For the first time since his arrival in camp, John was unable to identify a bird. This was very exciting because, as one of the foremost authorities on Neotropical birds, he knew every species of South American bird. Yet he was unable to name this one.

One of the birds was dead; the other was in weakened condition. I sensed that this was an extremely significant discovery, and I thought I should not ask what I was thinking, but I eventually did so anyway.

"John, can I photograph it in my bird tent?" I asked softly. Without saying a word, he gently handed me the bird.

"Don't let this one get away," Pete cautioned, because a bird had escaped from my photography tent earlier that week—my only loss of the expedition. The parrotlet was getting weaker by the moment, so I wasted no time in getting my photographs. Because this might indeed be a new species, nearly everyone in camp took advantage of the situation and also photographed the bird. By sunset, after John had gone over the possibilities in his mind, he made the announcement that all biologists wish they could utter: "It's new to science." Of course, without looking at comparative material back at LSU and without examining a male (both birds collected that day were females), he could not be 100 percent certain. But after all, this was John O'Neill, and nobody doubted the outcome for a moment.

The hour was getting late, and Don and I packed up loose ends. I still had a fair number of preserved specimens to label, record, and store in large plastic containers. My work took me late into the night. As I crawled into my tent for the last time, my flashlight caught a familiar but disturbing image. Ants were *everywhere*. Although these were not army ants or even leaf-cutter ants, they made their presence known. The main stream seemed to be coming from my camera bag. But why? I did not keep any food there for the obvious reason—there were just too many ants in and around camp.

A quick search of my camera case proved me wrong. In one of the compartments I found a chocolate bar. This was no ordinary chocolate. It was a local Peruvian brand that Donna told me about while passing time in the Lima airport. "This is Angelo's favorite," she explained. Since I consider myself a chocolate *aficionado*, I bought half a dozen of these cocoa treats to experience the best Peru had to offer. I was not disappointed. But the treat now in my hand was even more special. Many times I had wanted to tear into and devour it; but no, I had been saving this one, not for my own selfish palate, but to express my thanks to Angelo for having invited me on this trip. I realize it was not an extravagant or valuable gift, but to me it had meant a great deal. I had intended to present it to him in the morning as I departed camp. Now that was impossible. With great regret, I threw the remnants deep into the woods and never mentioned it again.

The next morning I was up early to prepare for my departure. Whenever I leave the tranquillity and solitude of the wild, I am always a bit depressed. This time was no different. After several weeks of productive and exciting herping adventures, it was time to say good-bye. Don and I collected everyone's mail and sundry notes and loaded our things into the *peki-peki*. After numerous group hugs and last minute farewells, we departed camp.

The water level in the river was higher than we had expected, and there was talk that we might arrive in Abujao that evening. About half a mile from camp, rounding a bend in the river, we came face to face with a young king vulture (*Sarcoramphus papa*) perched on a log overhanging the river. Surprisingly, it did not fly away, so with my camera handy, I took the last wildlife photo of the trip.

We arrived in Abujao as the sun was setting, sending red, orange, and purple streaks over the vast sky. It was most fitting that my final picture of the trip was of this unforgettably spectacular sight. We bid thanks and farewell to our guide, Oscar, who had transported us from a world where few dare to go, back into the reality of everyday life. As we left, I handed him a small stack of money with instructions that he buy a case of soft drinks and beer and deliver them to our friends at camp. After a month of river water, coffee, and hot chocolate, I imagined the gang was ready to celebrate the Fourth of July in style.

• •

John's suspicions proved correct. When he compared the newly collected parrotlets (now represented by a dozen specimens of both sexes) in the Lima Museum to all other similar birds back at LSU, he discovered that they were indeed new to science. They differed slightly from members of the *Forpus* group and subsequently were placed in the genus *Nannopsittaca,* which now doubles the number of species in that genus and increases the number of Peruvian parrots from forty-nine to fifty.

John and his ornithological colleagues Charles Munn and Irma Franke ultimately called the Amazonian parrotlet by the scientic name *Nannopsittaca dachilleae.* The specific epithet was chosen in honor of their dear friend Barbara D'Achille for dedicating her life to conservation efforts throughout South America.

CHAPTER 6

Time Traveling to Madagascar

A Look Back to Our Future

IN 1895 H. G. WELLS penned his classic novel *The Time Machine;* it was considered top-notch science fiction at the time and is still hailed as a significant piece of literature. During that period, the subject of time travel may have bordered on fantasy, but the truth is that time travel has been a reality for many years. Think about it. You board an airplane in your hometown, settle into your reclining seat, eat a few meals, and watch a movie. Within hours, you are transported to a remote region where the local inhabitants differ in appearance, customs, and behavior. In many cases, they lack even the most basic amenities on which you have grown to depend. You feel as though you have literally traveled back in time. Nowhere else did I find this experience more profound than on the island of Madagascar.

The mere mention of the name *Madagascar* usually evokes an instant nod of recognition, coupled with a wry smile. Although many people are unfamiliar with its exact location and even fewer have actually traveled there, this country (the world's fourth largest island) is often considered the globe's greatest natural resource in terms of wildlife biodiversity.

Located some 250 miles off the southeastern coast of Africa, this 1,000-mile-long "minicontinent" is believed to have broken away from the mainland about 100 million to 150 million years ago. As a result, nearly all of its flora and fauna has evolved in complete isolation, creating the highest percentage of plant and animal endemism anywhere on earth. Most of the species there occur nowhere else.

Even since the beginning of human habitation on the island—nearly two thousand years ago—Madagascar seemed destined for fame. Among the many discoveries made by the island natives were dozens of giant lemurs (prosimianlike primates), huge tortoises, and the elephant bird, the largest bird ever to roam the earth. Sadly, with the arrival of "civilization," humankind began its exploitation of Madagascar's natural resources. As a result, all these species, and many more, have long since been eliminated from the island.

In late 1988, Madagascar opened its doors to the world by announcing that it would allow, on a trial basis, limited research projects designed to encourage scientists, naturalists, and tourists to visit the island to generate sorely needed funds for the country's impoverished economy. Madagascar soon became a popular travel destination. As a result, the early nineties produced inspiring nature shows and documentaries about this unique land. In reality, however, not all has been going well for the island. For the past several decades, Madagascar has been losing enormous tracts of land to the country's "slash and burn" agriculture (*tavy*, in their native language). This practice of cutting down the forests and burning the remaining vegetation has caused severe soil erosion that prevents plants from regrowing, thus creating a permanent loss of habitat. Vegetation maps, compared over the past fifty years, clearly show that much of the country's original rain forest has disappeared. By current estimates, only about 5 to 10 percent of original rain forest remains, and most of what is left will probably be destroyed in the near future. Contemplating these grim statistics, many tourists and naturalists are making a concerted effort to see Madagascar before its riches have vanished.

••

Unlike my visits to other parts of the world, which were usually made in conjunction with institutions or organizations, I planned my trip to Madagascar as a private venture with three friends who were equally impassioned to see the island. Debbie, Joe, and Gary had all attended my previous travelogues and were anxious to participate in one of my adventures—

not vicariously—but "in person." After nearly half a year of making contacts with experienced travelers and acquiring equipment, literature, and various supplies, we made plans to arrive in Madagascar in mid-May of 1989.

Since the country only recently (in 1960) gained its independence from France, one of its two main languages is French. The other language is Malagasy, a local dialect from the Malayo-Polynesian family of languages. Using my rusty French from high school and college classes taken twenty years earlier, I was surprised that we managed as well as we did.

Before landing in Madagascar, I studied a map of the island to better acquaint myself with the country's geography. It soon became evident that city names in Madagascar are often long and difficult to pronounce. Furthermore, most towns have two names: the old colonial name and a traditional Malagasy one. The capital, Antananarivo, was fortunately shortened to the unofficial name "Tana," although other cities throughout the country remain even more unpronounceable: tongue-twisters like Fiana-rantsoa, Ambatondrazaka, Tsinjomitondraka, and Antetezampandrana, to name a few. Even surnames of local residents are nearly impossible to pronounce: Andrianiantefana, Rondrianosolo, and Razafintsialonina, for example. Early inhabitants also had long names. In the late eighteenth century, a Malagasy king was called Andrianampoinimerinandriant-simitoviaminandriampanjaka. To the delight of many of his subjects, this was later "shortened" to just the first twenty letters.

• •

Our flight from the United States took us on a roundabout route to Mada-gascar, with a ten-hour stopover in France and a twenty-four-hour lay-over in Kenya, before we finally landed in Tana. The taxi ride from the Tana airport allowed us to see the entire city from a distance and to get a view of the king's palace. By law, the palace must be the tallest structure in Madagascar, and photographing it is forbidden unless appropriate documents are first obtained. (When our driver saw me taking pictures of it as we drove into the city, he nearly threw me out of his vehicle.)

With the driver's assistance, we found a modest hotel and secured several rooms that we used as a "base camp." Because we planned to stay in the capital only a day or two while awaiting a rental vehicle, we were not too concerned about our accommodations. The rooms were small, run-down, and sparsely furnished. There was only one toilet in the building, and it had no door and no toilet paper. I was warned in advance about the toilets in Madagascar and also cautioned about their "toilet paper." When

View of the *zoma* marketplace in Madagascar's capital, Antananarivo (Tana).

it was available, which was virtually never, it had the consistency of cardboard and the absorbency of aluminum foil. Anticipating this, I had brought a supply of toilet paper from the United States and was told by a number of people that I could trade a single roll for any of the local woodcarvings, textiles, jewelry, or even protected wildlife.

The lack of toilets notwithstanding, we were pleased by the spectacular view from our rooms. At the north end of town were old brick homes made from the rich, red soil commonly seen throughout Madagascar. The southern view revealed an old train station amidst several of the "newer," more modern hotels. What we did not know at the time was that the entire area was about to blossom into the world's largest outdoor marketplace, the *zoma*. *Zoma* is an Arabic word meaning "Friday," the day on which the market reaches its zenith, in terms of size. Although it is a veritable beehive of activity all week long, the busiest day is Friday, when merchants come from all over the country to sell their wares. Except for the night before *zoma*, when construction kept us awake into the wee hours of the morning, we felt lucky to have perfectly timed our arrival to coincide with this incredible experience. Thousands of stalls stretched from one end of town to the other, each with a large, white umbrella sheltering the vendors and their goods. Since poverty in the country is among the worst anywhere, some had very little to sell. (Average per capita income in Madagascar is a paltry $175 to $250 a year.) A few vendors sat in the intense heat all day long just to sell a handful of potatoes, while others offered to sell car parts from 1959 Peugeots, the last year that France imported automobiles or car parts into the country. (This *zoma* is no longer extant, having been disbanded in the early 1990s.)

The most disturbing part of the experience was the large number of people who tried to sell Madagascar's wildlife. Many booths displayed mounted butterflies and moths in glass picture frames, while others exploited the reptile fauna. Dozens of vendors offered belts, wallets, and purses made from skins of the local snakes, including a gaudy pair of lady's boots fabricated from the skins of the protected Dumeril's ground boa *(Boa [Acrantophis] dumerili)*. Other atrocities included model sailboats crafted from shells of the endangered radiated tortoise *(Geochelone radiata)* and ashtrays fashioned from the feet of juvenile Nile crocodiles *(Crocodilus niloticus)*. As I walked through this busy and crowded fairground, I was quickly overwhelmed by the kaleidoscope of strange sights, smells, and sounds of this "umbrella jungle." Hundreds of scantily clad children roamed the streets begging for coins or food from tourists and locals alike. Some tried to appear more pitiful than they really were. One small boy smeared ketchup on his leg and walked with an exaggerated limp, pretending to have suffered a severe injury. After we offered him a few coins, he skipped away, giggling and singing in French. Another young boy tried to sell us a hatchling radiated tortoise for thirty-five cents. (Captive-hatched specimens in the United States sell for several thousand dollars each.) All tortoises in Madagascar are strictly protected and neither collecting nor exporting permits are issued, even for research purposes.

Knowing we would be able to shop again later on our trip, we delayed purchasing souvenirs until close to our departure. Now our task was to find someone from whom we could rent a vehicle to take us around Madagascar. As luck would have it, a young man approached us while we dined in the hotel restaurant and asked whether we needed a vehicle. When we

Reptile-skin products in the marketplace of Madagascar's capital, Antananarivo, or "Tana."

explained to him that we wanted to visit as much of the island as possible in three weeks, he offered to drive us to the southeast, south, and southwest regions of the country. There was only one catch: we would have to travel with a small group of European tourists who would accompany us in a separate car. Since the cost for this excursion seemed reasonable, we accepted his offer. Pleased with our good fortune, we were anxious to start the trip; but then came the bad news: it would be a few days before we could leave. Meanwhile, the driver took us to the local zoo to meet some of the country's top herpetologists, ornithologists, and mammalogists. As a "zoo person," I am always anxious to visit foreign zoos to learn more about the indigenous fauna of those countries.

• •

The Tsimbazaza Zoo was spacious, even by U.S. standards. Its roughly seventy-five acres contained a number of fine animal exhibits. The entry fee was a mere pittance, and our group contributed some additional money as a gesture of goodwill from the Houston Zoo to theirs. We also had Houston Zoo tee shirts with us that we left as gifts for each of the curators. Our timing was terrible, however, since most of the administrative staff were gone from the zoo and would not be back for two days. To our disappointment, the reptile building was closed. With my broken French, I asked two of the zoo's gardeners when we would be able to get inside to see the animals. Without saying a word, one of them produced a key and opened the building. For their kindness, we gave the two men a pack of U.S. cigarettes. Their eyes grew wide at this token gift, and they almost fell to their knees over what they perceived as an extravagant present.

The animals in this small building were mostly reptiles, but several of the cages contained indigenous mammals. Among the more notable creatures were three species of chameleons, a few Dumeril's ground boas, several day geckos, and the island's most dominant predatory mammal, the fossa (pronounced "foosh"), *Cryptoprocta ferox*. Resembling a short-legged cat, this endemic carnivore is related to the civets and mongooses of neighboring Africa. Although seldom exceeding twenty pounds, these agile climbers are the main predators of the island's lemurs.

Though the exhibits were prepared without substrate and little in the way of plants, tree limbs, or shelter, the animals seemed in surprisingly good health. Except for several giant tortoises from Aldabra Island, nearly all of the displayed animals occur in Madagascar. Much to our delight, we saw lined day geckos (*Phelsuma lineata*), various "treefrogs" (*Boophis* sp.), and even an introduced gecko *(Hemidactylus mabouia)* living wild on the zoo grounds.

In one of the buildings an educational exhibit displayed mounted and preserved examples of Madagascar's wildlife. Of the twenty-nine species of lemurs known to occur on the island (at that time), nearly half were represented there, along with dozens of bird species, including the skeleton of an elephant bird, the largest bird that ever lived. Next to it was the skeleton of an ostrich, showing its diminutive size by comparison. Nestled at the base of the elephant bird's feet was an enormous, intact egg of the species, which was somewhat larger than a football.

In a large six-foot-long aquarium, devoid of any preservative fluid, was the most intriguing item of all: a shriveled, mummified coelacanth *(Latimeria chalumnae)*. This legendary fish, thought to have been extinct for fifty million years, was "rediscovered" in 1938 by a fisherman who caught a specimen off the northeastern coast of South Africa. It was hailed as the find of the century, but no other specimens were collected until 1952. Several of these primitive, lobed-fin fish were subsequently caught in the 1950s near the Comoro Islands. For several minutes, I stared in awe at the sight, well aware of the animal's significance. It was a shame that this specimen, one of the rarest of all fishes, was allowed to decompose and finally rot because the museum was simply unable to afford the formaldehyde necessary to keep the fish in good condition. (Recently, small numbers of coelacanths have been observed in and sometimes collected from the Madagascar Channel area as well as the Comoro Islands; a new species also was accidentally discovered in Indonesia.)

••

After visiting the zoo, we exchanged our U.S. dollars for the local currency, the Malagasy franc (Fmg). The entire process was pure chaos. Numerous forms had to be filled out (by us and by bank employees), several bank executives were called in to witness the exchange of money, and we had to show all our U.S. currency to the bank officials. We were told that upon our departure from Madagascar, all the money we exchanged, plus any remaining monies, must add up to the exact amount we declared when we entered the country. This was to discourage black market dealings, which were strictly prohibited.

The current rate of exchange was Fmg 1650 to one U.S. dollar. This meant that changing more than $600 U.S. made you an instant Malagasy millionaire. Given that their largest denomination bill at the time was

Fmg 10,000 (approximately $6), we ended up with pockets bulging to capacity with local currency.

Any time we traveled within the city, we hired a taxi. The cost of taxi transportation was reasonable; most trips cost less than fifty cents (for all of us). Nearly all taxis were in a terrible state of repair, and we were required to pay the fare up front, not because the driver feared we would skip out without paying, but because the driver had to purchase the gasoline in advance. Again, the degree of poverty in the country was so pronounced that most drivers could not afford to fill their gas tanks, so they had to purchase gasoline before setting out, even on short trips. We were especially concerned when we saw how they "filled" their tanks. Sitting on the front seat between the driver and the passenger was a plastic, two-liter soft drink bottle into which the driver poured the gasoline. A small hose connected this bottle to the gas tank, thus allowing a steady trickle of fuel to drip into the engine. Each time we entered a taxi, we literally took our lives into our hands.

Another mode of transportation was the *pousse-pousse*, or rickshaw. This was a safer way to travel but much slower. The cost of hiring one of these "vehicles" was only ten cents, and with a generous tip, you could spend as much as a quarter per trip.

• •

Our local tour guide, Philippe Morlet, a Frenchman, had established a local car rental business in the capital several years ago. He seemed interested in our activities and was fascinated to learn that we had come to Madagascar specifically to collect reptiles and amphibians in order to study their parasites. Philippe apparently was well connected, and the day before our departure he took us to the local museum and introduced us to Dr. Charles Domergue, the leading authority on Malagasy snakes, who has described more than thirty new species in recent years. Although he was seventy-eight years old at the time, Dr. Domergue was in much better physical shape than I. He admitted to drinking two liters of wine a day, smoking one to two packs of cigarettes daily, walking three miles to and from his house, and having a twenty-four-year-old girlfriend. There was no way I could keep up with him, either in the field or socially. He told us there were many species of reptiles and amphibians in the museum gardens, and he welcomed us to return at night to search for them. He also had a substantial number of live indigenous herps in his office and allowed us the opportunity to examine and photograph them at our leisure. Because his English

The author meets the spry, seventy-eight-year-old Dr. Charles Domergue, Madagascar's leading authority on local snakes.

was nearly nonexistent and my French just as weak, we communicated through scientific terms and hand gestures. Dr. Domergue made one more generous offer: to house and feed any animals we found until our departure nearly a month later. This really helped since we eventually collected more specimens than we could have cared for in the field.

That night we visited his facility, where we wandered the grounds and caught our first chameleon: a short-horned, or elephant-ear, chameleon *(Calumma [Chamaeleo] brevicornis)*. Males have a short nasal appendage that is lacking in females. Also, when provoked, a male extends and waves his large occipital lobes, which lie on either side of his head, giving him the look of a miniature elephant flapping its ears in a menacing way. Madagascar has the world's greatest diversity of chameleons, with nearly two-thirds of the 160 known species found exclusively on the island.

• •

The following afternoon we met Philippe at the airport. The flight from Tana to the southeastern village of Fort Dauphin was less than two hours, but from the moment we took off to the time we landed, the condition of the terrain was disturbing. There were virtually no trees, although at one time most of the region had been heavily forested. We also saw muddy rivers awash with reddish silt from the barren hillsides. During the rainy season, when most rivers are engorged with runoff from the deforested hills, the aerial view makes Madagascar look as though it is slowly bleeding to death—a haunting and depressing sight.

We arrived in Fort Dauphin an hour before sunset. This coastal town is blessed with clean, pristine beaches and sizable tracts of dense forest.

Upon landing, we saw numerous chickens and dogs on the tarmac, seemingly oblivious to the rush of people around them. After we deplaned, we walked a short distance to the "baggage recovery" area, where our luggage was stacked on a rickety old cart parked on a grassy area next to the terminal. Here, the departing passengers would grab their luggage before leaving the airport. With no one to check claim stubs, we were certain that half our belongings would be stolen, but to our pleasant surprise, none of our baggage was missing.

At the airport we were met by two of Philippe's vehicles. Along with five European guests with whom we would share our adventure, we were driven to a nearby hotel, where we unloaded our belongings. The sun was getting low on the horizon, and not wanting to waste even one minute, we excused ourselves from the group and began our initial herping adventure down along the beach. The weather was glorious, with temperatures in the mid-eighties. On the beach we found numerous logs and rocks, under which we hoped to find something reptilian. Our first find was a juvenile gecko, *Paroedura bastardi.* Unfortunately, many of Madagascar's reptiles and amphibians have no common names, but based upon its scientific name, this particular gecko might appropriately be referred to as the "bastard" gecko. As I exposed the tiny lizard from under its shelter, it squeaked faintly, then stood on its tiptoes to make itself look bigger. Next, we found a Brahminy blind snake *(Ramphotyphlops braminus),* a species not native to the island but one that has been introduced worldwide via the potted-plant trade. This is a tiny, subterranean snake only four to six inches long and about as thick as the lead in a pencil. It is to date, the world's only known parthenogenic snake; that is, only females of the species exist. Several lizards share this strange characteristic in which reproduction takes place without benefit of the male's sperm, although none were known to occur in Madagascar at the time of my visit. (A dwarf gecko, *Lygodactylus pauliani,* described in 1991, is known from only eight females. This may in fact now represent parthenogenesis in Malagasy lizards.) Ten species of blind snakes are found on Madagascar; one is named after Dr. Domergue.

We were back at the hotel just after sunset, but before checking into my room, I searched around the compound for wildlife. In addition to several treefrogs in the genus *Boophis,* I found a house gecko *(Hemidactylus frenatus)* on the side of a tree. The gecko was so well camouflaged that it was nearly impossible to see. One of the frogs, *B. pauliani,* a pale luminescent green amphibian, resembled a piece of rare oriental jade.

With the group waiting to begin dinner until I arrived, I finally made an appearance in the dining room. This was more a social gathering than anything else, giving everyone a chance to become better acquainted. Fortunately, all the Europeans spoke English. Two couples were from France, and a third gentleman was a resident of Mauritius Island (in the Mascarene Island chain, east of Madagascar).

After dinner, I asked whether we could take one of the vehicles to search for reptiles and amphibians in a nearby forest we had seen from the plane. Philippe did not feel comfortable loaning us one of the cars but said that he would allow one of the drivers to take us to the woods and return to pick us up several hours later. That arrangement suited us fine, and soon we were on our way.

The driver left us at the site, which was not far from the hotel, and agreed to come back at midnight, giving us nearly six hours to herp. The four of us were excited finally to be in a Madagascan forest away from people, civilization, and other similar distractions. Minutes after our arrival, Debbie called us over to a tree where she had found a beautiful Malagasy cat-eyed snake *(Madagascarophis colubrinus)* sleeping in a knothole. At first glance, this serpent appears venomous: it has elliptical eye pupils like many venomous species and an "arrow-shaped" head. Although a member of the colubrid family (the "harmless" snakes), the reptile possesses a mild venom that is delivered through enlarged, grooved teeth at the rear of the snake's mouth. The bite is harmless to humans, however, and serves merely to subdue its lizard prey.

What many Madagascan locals do not understand is that there are *no* dangerously venomous snakes on Madagascar. Despite this, they kill all snakes on sight (a senseless act that occurs worldwide) unless they are from a tribe that considers killing a snake *fady*, or taboo. Malagasy people follow different rules concerning *fady*, depending upon which tribe they represent (there are eighteen tribes in Madagascar). For example, some believe it is *fady* to eat certain foods, some will not work the fields or hold a funeral on certain days of the week, while others consider it *fady* to hand an egg directly to another person before first placing it on the ground.

Joe, who is extremely fond of geckos, became highly animated when he found an endemic gecko sitting on the leaf of a small bush. His prize was a diminutive species known as *Ebenavia inunguis*, a tiny lizard with a pointed head, a black-and-white-banded tail, and a series of small spines scattered along its back and tail. Although it was neither colorful nor dramatic looking, Joe was thrilled with his find.

Gary made a significant discovery when he spotted a chameleon high up in a tree. We had no idea how we would capture it; it was at least thirty to forty feet off the ground. Both Joe and Gary climbed the tree hoping to bend the branch down far enough for someone on the ground to reach it. With Debbie and me shining our flashlights on the chameleon (and on the two acrobats), Gary and Joe somehow miraculously captured the lizard. After much cheering, we all examined the animal but could not identify it. In 1989, there were no herpetological field guides with color photographs and range maps to help us identify indigenous wildlife. All we had was a 1943 work by the French herpetologist Angel (pronounced On-jell) which was in French and had some of the chameleon species sketched in black-and-white. In addition, we had with us a 1971 paper by another French herpetologist, Dr. E. R. Brygoo, which also concerned Malagasy chameleons. It too was in French. Since then, a number of excellent wildlife guides have been published, most of them in English, which include descriptions of many of the numerous wildlife species discovered since the 1970s.

With Angel's key, we determined the specimen we had was the third largest chameleon species in Madagascar, the "giant-spiny" chameleon (*Furcifer [Chamaeleo] verrucosus*). Like most chameleons, this species is sexually dimorphic: males differ from females either by size or coloration. Our specimen, a female, was orange with small spines along her back. Later that night, we caught several more females and a few males, which were bigger (by 20 to 30 percent) and had much larger spines along their backs and tails. When two males came close to one another, their coloration changed dramatically to a bright chartreuse green on the lower halves of their bodies and grayish black with white stripes above. Like nearly all chameleon species, male *Furcifer verrucosus* do not tolerate the presence of other males, even if they are just passing by.

By midnight, after having collected numerous lizards, frogs, and several snakes, we were exhausted and ready to return to the hotel. Our driver met us at the agreed upon time and within minutes we were back in our rooms, examining the night's catch. Even though I was tired, I still had a lot of work to do. I had brought with me numerous empty milk cartons in which to house chameleons temporarily. By placing one lizard in each container, I could keep them from becoming agitated at seeing one another, and I could inscribe the appropriate collecting data for each specimen directly on the carton. I followed this routine with every animal. After placing them in individual containers, I then stored the cartons in a large mesh diving bag (so the animals would have access to fresh air). We also followed this technique when we were on the road, hanging the mesh bags inside the center of the vehicle in order to protect the animals from the direct rays of the sun and to provide them with fresh, moving air. We took fecal samples daily to check for parasites and then placed the samples in small vials containing a solution of potassium dichromate. Once back in the United States, we would send the fecal samples to various collaborators to be checked microscopically for parasites.

The next morning we loaded all our belongings into one of the jeeps. Our vehicle was full of collecting gear, containers, camera equipment, and personal belongings; the other vehicle had baggage piled on the roof, leaving the passengers room inside to stretch out and enjoy the ride. By midmorning we were on our way to the southwestern part of the island, a region known as the "spiny desert."

As we approached the desert, we could see an abrupt change in the vegetation and wildlife from that of the forests we had left behind. The flora here is different, too, from that of the rest of Madagascar. Tall cactuslike plants in the Didieraceae and Euphorbiaceae families dominate the landscape. Some plants, such as those in the genus *Alluaudia*, sometimes referred to as octopus trees, are forty-five to fifty feet tall, spindly, and adorned with spiral rows of huge thorns. These are favorite plants of the sifaka lemurs (pronounced she-faak), whose thick, tough foot pads allow them to climb the wobbly, springy stalks without injury.

A number of plants are unique to Madagascar. One, the traveler palm (*Ravenala madagascariensis*), has an interesting history. When the first settlers came to the island, they discovered that the leaves of these thirty- to forty-five-foot-tall plants contain a significant amount of water. Before setting out on a journey, or during a long trek, the natives cut the enormous leaves from the base of the plant and carried them along. By holding the base of the giant leaf above their mouths, they could obtain a substantial amount of refreshing, relatively clean water.

The island is also known for its production of vanilla, *Vanilla planifolia*, 90 percent of which, when processed, is exported to the United States. Although the primary plant used for export was originally introduced from Mexico, four additional species are native to Madagascar.

Perhaps the best-known endemic plant is the rosy periwinkle (*Cantharanthus roseus*), a species containing two alkaloid chemicals used effectively to treat childhood leukemia as well as certain other cancers. Although this ornamental plant has long been exported worldwide, it is now cultivated on most other continents.

Our drive through southwestern Madagascar took us along National Route 10, which was little more than a series of interconnected holes in the red Malagasy earth. In fact, the ruts in this one-lane "road" were so deep and treacherous that most of the time we had to swerve off the pathway and drive on the road's edge at speeds averaging ten miles per hour. It took us the better part of an entire day to go about seventy-five miles.

As we made our way north, we could see the beautiful blue waters of the Indian Ocean and the sugary white sands of the deserted beaches. Just before sunset, our driver made an abrupt stop in the middle of the road, causing us to lurch forward and sending most of our baggage cascading on top of us. The unexpected stop proved wise, however, as we had nearly run over a radiated tortoise. Ever since I had worked with this species at the Houston Zoo, I desperately wanted to see a wild specimen. We all piled out of the car to stare in awe at this magnificent creature. Its black, high-domed shell covered with bright yellow radiating lines was characteristic of the species. We immediately pulled out our cameras and video equipment and began to take pictures, carrying on as though we had encountered an extraterrestrial being. After examining it, we carried the fifteen-inch-long, half-grown tortoise to safety, some fifty feet from the road, for we were concerned that another passing car might run over it. (Our precautions were unnecessary because we saw no other vehicles on this road for days.)

Later, we encountered a second specimen of this endangered tortoise, again in the middle of the road. Despite our thorough examination of the first animal, we lavished our attention on this one as well before turning it loose in the nearby desert. In the next few days, we encountered several dozen more radiated tortoises, but it was only after seeing about twenty-five of them that we began to view them with a more blasé attitude.

We made camp near a pristine beach, and while we set up our tents, our guides prepared a delicious meal of chicken, rice, and local vegetables. As we sat around the campfire eating dinner, we chatted with our European guests, discussing our goals for the expedition. Although fascinated with details of our work, they were not looking forward to the prospect of our capturing snakes. When I explained that no venomous snakes occur on the island, they seemed relieved.

After dinner, Debbie, Joe, Gary, and I went out into the night to search for herps. In this coastal environment, we did not expect to find amphibians since they are intolerant of saltwater. Reptiles, however, can tolerate saltwater. Flipping over debris near the beach, we discovered a three-inch-long fish-scaled gecko *(Geckolepis typica)*, one of half a dozen species of this genus in Madagascar, all of which share characteristic overlapping body scales like those of most fish.

Along the beach we unexpectedly came upon a macabre sight. In a two-foot-deep hole near the water we found several dozen shells and skulls of radiated tortoises, evidently victims of human activity. The image was disturbing, and we wondered who would commit such an atrocity against these gentle creatures. At camp, we told the guides about our discovery, and they all nodded in recognition. They indicated that because radiated tortoises are considered a delicacy in Madagascar, they are frequently eaten by many of the locals despite their protected status. This demonstrates again the hypocrisy of the conservation ethic as it is practiced in many countries. Although Madagascar prohibits collection or exportation of this endangered species, indigenous people are allowed to eat as many of them as they wish. This practice is not limited just to the average person; I even witnessed a high-ranking official killing radiated tortoises.

One evening, as we gathered around the campfire for dinner, one of the European women in the group noticed that her purse was missing. Because it contained her passport and most of her money, she was frantic over the loss. The next morning we went to the nearest town to report the theft to a police officer. As we approached the policeman's home, we saw that he was bending over a cooking pot with a large knife in his hand. A closer look revealed that he was cutting up a radiated tortoise, so without being obvious, I quickly raised my camera and took a picture of him. Despite my nervousness while taking the picture, it turned out fairly well, and even the officer's badge can be clearly seen in the photo. We reported the purse theft, and perhaps as a result of a rumor started by the authorities that a great misfortune would befall whoever had stolen it, both the purse and the money it contained were anonymously returned a day later.

Our routine was the same every day: we drove along nonexistent roads by day, eventually finding a place to camp by sunset. Despite the area's remoteness, within minutes of stopping to camp or rest, we ended up surrounded by the local people. Sometimes entire villages gathered around just to sit and stare while we went about our daily routines. Their attention to everything we did was amusing at first, but eventually the constant scrutiny became annoying.

Early one morning I awoke to begin the day's routine of catching insects to feed our growing collection of lizards and to photograph the previous day's catch. When I unzipped my tent, I was surprised to see several

In a remote village in southwestern Madagascar, a local village chief and his son watch intently as our group goes through its daily routine in the early morning.

dozen natives scattered throughout our campsite. Standing a few feet from my tent were the village chief and his young son. The chief, who was holding a five-foot-long spear, stared at our guides as they prepared breakfast, which offered me a great photo opportunity. These frequent visits became extremely awkward, especially when one of us needed to answer nature's call. Since no "facilities" were available, we were obligated to sneak off into the bush to accomplish our business, each time followed by several curious natives. This often resulted in an aborted mission. Sometimes I had to pull a chameleon or snake out of a pillowcase and entertain the crowd, thus allowing some group members to eventually slip away to relieve themselves.

Because many of the natives in these small, remote communities had never seen a white person, the children often ran to Debbie to touch her golden hair and stroke her pale skin. At first, she considered the constant attention endearing, but soon the often-repeated ritual became irritating.

Once when we were low on fuel, we stopped in a tiny village to purchase gasoline. Within a few minutes, the local chief invited us all to his home, where we were treated to a fantastic meal prepared in our honor. When he asked what we were doing in the area, we replied that we were conducting scientific research on reptiles. In response, he assembled most of the residents and instructed them (in Malagasy) to go out and search for lizards and snakes and bring them back to us alive. Most people worldwide have a natural fear of snakes, and the Malagasy are no exception, but when a village chief gives an order, it is followed without question. As we dined, locals began to appear with all kinds of lizards and snakes. Some collectors were innovative and used pieces of plastic and burlap bags to contain the animals; others simply tied a piece of string around a lizard's foot or a snake's midsection and dragged the reptiles to us. The lizards were mostly spiny-tailed iguanas, *Oplurus cyclurus,* and the smaller endemic oplurine iguanid *Chalarodon madagascariensis.*

The presence on this island of iguanid lizards raises an interesting scientific question: why are there iguanas on Madagascar when there are no representatives nearby on mainland Africa? The same question can be asked about the three species of endemic boas. Finally, we wonder why so many snake and lizard families (for example, vipers, elapids, agamids, and monitors) occur in Africa but not in Madagascar. Some researchers speculate that many millions of years ago when all the continents were still joined together as the supercontinent Gondwanaland, several land bridges enabled *some* of the wildlife to pass from one region to the other.

Most of the snakes collected by the natives were small colubrids, all of them nondescript and with no common names: *Dromicodryas bernieri, Mimophis mahfalensis,* and *Liophidium vallanti.*

We were indebted to our host for his gracious hospitality, and before leaving we presented him with gifts of soap, candy, and batteries. Despite the welcome additions to our herpetological collection, I was pleased to be back on the road and away from well-meaning crowds.

Itampolo, the next village on our route along the southwestern coast of the island, actually appears on the national map of Madagascar. The village consisted of three barely standing huts and a slightly sturdier structure that appeared to be a church (its roof was adorned with what looked like a cross). Since it was almost sundown, we decided to camp there for the night. As I ambled over to the huts, I could see many fish lined up on wooden racks, drying in the last rays of the sun. Scattered about in the white sand around the huts were half a dozen large sea turtle shells. As I bent down to examine one, a few of the villagers came over to watch. Although we were unable to communicate with each other, they sensed that I was curious about the source of the shells. In Malagasy, they instructed me to follow them a short distance to the shoreline where they showed me the boat they used to search for fish and turtles at sea. The rickety, hand-carved vessel was made from the trunk of the famous baobab tree, a bizarre-looking species that Malagasy lore says was created by God in anger. In His wrath, He supposedly pulled the trees from the earth and stuck them back in upside down, creating the illusion that the root system grows at the top of the tree and not in the ground. In all of Africa, there is only a single species of baobab; Madagascar has eight.

One of the men motioned for me to follow him to a place where a young boy stood guard over a live sea turtle tethered by a rope around its front flippers. I was both mesmerized and horrified. I knew full well the fate of this unfortunate turtle, and I knew there was nothing I could do to stop it. The boy was standing with his arms clasped behind his back. To me, the image it created was powerful and symbolic. Here was a turtle bound by its "arms," while a boy with his arms "missing" was assigned to watch over it. When the elderly man invited us to participate with him and his villagers in celebrating the night's feast, I became even more depressed. We politely declined the invitation but thanked him for his kind offer.

• •

In southwestern Madagascar we occasionally encountered large, square-shaped, human-made structures fashioned from hand-chiseled stones. These are the tombs or crypts of the *Mahafaly* (pronounced Ma-ha-faal) people. Most Malagasy believe that death is not the final step in a person's life but is merely a transition to another life. The *Mahafaly* construct elaborate tombs into which they place deceased family members, together with their personal belongings. Tombs are often ornately decorated with zebu horns as well as intricate wood carvings (usually depicting events in the person's life), pottery, colorful fabrics, and even jewelry. To most Malagasy people, zebus (a large breed of cattle with an exaggerated hump behind the head) are not consumed as food but are used as sacrifices should

Malagasy child
guarding endangered
sea turtle intended
for village meal in
southwestern
Madagascar.

a *fady* be broken. The accumulation of many zebus is, therefore, considered a symbol of wealth and power. Impoverished people who own no cattle can afford to decorate their family tombs with only a single pair of horns, and I even saw one humble tomb where, instead of an actual pair of zebu horns, a tree branch was carved into the shape of horns.

Funeral practices of Malagasy people vary from one tribe to another, but the best-known ceremony in Madagascar is called *famadihana* (pronounced fam-a-dee-an), literally, "turning of the bones." Several years after a person dies, family members celebrate the life of the deceased by removing the corpse from the tomb, carrying it several times around the burial site, showing it any additions or improvements to the town, and talking to it. At the conclusion of this gala event, the bones are rewrapped in a new burial shroud *(lamba mena)* and carried around the tomb before being placed back inside.

Surrounding these crypts are rocks of different sizes, a likely place to find herpetological specimens. While I would not desecrate or remove these sacred objects from the immediate vicinity of the burial sites, the opportunity to look for reptiles there was too great to ignore. We made certain that we moved no rocks located less than twenty feet from these structures. In a relatively short time, we had collected some unique and very interesting specimens. One was a legless skink *(Voeltzkowia [Grandiderina] lineata)*. Full grown, this species is only four inches long and not much thicker than pencil lead. Nearly blind, it spends most of its time underground in search of small invertebrates, its preferred prey. My catch was

Mahafaly tribal tomb in southwest Madagascar adorned with zebu horns and wooden carvings.

easy to find but difficult to keep from escaping. When I held it in my hand, it burrowed between my fingers and fell to the ground, where it immediately tried to bury itself in the soft sand. I lost it several times, only to find it again after a frantic search through six-inch-deep sand.

As we searched among the rocks and bushes, Joe called me over to see something unusual he had just caught. Initially hiding his prize from me, he slowly pulled his hand from behind his back to reveal a beautiful, four-inch-long adult spider tortoise *(Pyxis arachnoides)*. I was stunned. I had hoped to see radiated tortoises in the wild but never for a moment thought we would be lucky enough to find one of these. Like their larger cousins, they are strictly protected, and permits for their export are just not issued. Due to their small size (they are considered one of the smallest tortoises in the world) and their colorful black-and-yellow carapace, they are highly prized by collectors and are thus in great demand on the black market, where adults typically sell for between two thousand and three thousand dollars each. We were later offered a hatchling of this species for twenty-five cents. Naturally, we declined.

Joe now expressed a desire to collect a radiated tortoise so he could have his picture taken with these two exquisite tortoise species. Thirty seconds later, Gary found one, and soon Joe and the tortoises were immortalized on film.

We continued our drive along the southwestern coast to the Lake Tsimanampetsotsa Nature Reserve. I quickly decided that "Tsimanampetsotsa" must be Malagasy for "land where mosquitoes drill into marrow," as this was the worst place in Madagascar for these annoying pests. We stopped to see some of the rare birds that live in this region, but spent most of our time trying to extricate our vehicle from a mud hole that our driver had failed to see. The second vehicle, which was some distance ahead of us, was not aware of our dilemma. After we had tried for fifteen minutes to free our truck, the other vehicle finally came back to help, but despite the strenuous efforts of the entire group, the car seemed cemented in place. As we pondered our next move, a young native appeared, seemingly from nowhere, wearing a World Wildlife Fund tee shirt. He informed us that because this was a nature reserve, we could not *park* here. We explained our situation, and soon, with his help, we pushed clear of the mud.

This region was designated a nature reserve not only because of the many exotic bird species found here, but also because it supports a unique species of fish. In a small cave containing a shallow pond, we observed nearly a dozen white blind cave fish *(Typhleotris madagascariensis)*, a rare endangered species found only in this cave system. Ironically, when I opened a termite mound at the cave entrance I found a pink, four-inch-long blind snake *(Typhlops arenarius)*, which, like all members of its family, lives underground and feeds entirely on ants and termites and their eggs.

Since we had no permits to collect here, we continued north to the sizable town of Tulear, where we decided to take a break from camping and spend a few days in a four-dollar-a-night "hotel." Although accommodations were humble, the hotel grounds were appealing. As soon as the sun had set, we walked around the compound to search for herps. Our first find was a large, twelve-inch-long male giant spiny chameleon *(Furcifer verrucosus)*. With our four flashlights converging on it, the reptile squinted at us in bewilderment. On the trunk of a nearby tree we saw another lizard—a species of day gecko that, unlike most other day geckos, is drab-looking instead of brightly colored. This was the somber-hued desert day gecko *(Phelsuma leiogaster)*. While our lights were trained up into the trees, I heard a slight rustling beneath the nearby leaf litter. As I shined my flashlight on the ground in the direction of the disturbance, I was stunned by what I saw. It was a terrestrial gecko that resembled a cross between a Central American elegant gecko *(Coleonyx elegans)* and a Namib sand gecko *(Chondrodactylus angulifer)*, and it was fast making its way through the leaves to freedom. I called to Joe to help me catch it, and with his and Debbie's assistance, we soon held a Malagasy ground gecko *(Paroedura pictus)* in our hands. Never having seen or heard of this species before, we were in awe of its beautiful pattern and impressed with its size (five inches long from tip to tip). Before the night was over we had caught five individuals, including one that had a pale stripe from behind its head to the tip of its tail, and a hatchling that looked entirely different from the adults.

At one point, Joe and I heard scratching sounds in the leaf litter, and when the mystery animal finally emerged, we were face-to-face with a spiny tenrec, a small hedgehoglike mammal covered with sharp spines. I abruptly yelled to Joe, "Quick, Joe, grab it!"

"Yeah, right," he quipped back. "You grab it!" Although it was not quite as scary as grabbing a porcupine, we both opted to play it safe and allow the prickly insectivore to continue on its way unmolested.

The next morning, Debbie woke up with what seemed like a bad cold; she had difficulty breathing and felt generally weak and tired. As we continued north, her condition worsened. We finally discovered the problem. Throughout the trip, we had been driving in the dry, sandy desert with the car windows open, and most of the red dust from this region ended up in the back of the vehicle where Debbie was sitting. Although we were all coated with a thick layer of dust, Debbie had apparently gotten the worst of it.

Just north of the coastal town of Ifaty, we stopped for lunch. Joe and Gary did some scuba diving in the ocean while Debbie and I went in search of reptiles. After trying in vain to keep up with me, she settled down in the shade of a tree and told me to go on without her because respiratory condition was worsening. Not feeling right about leaving her behind, I informed our guide of her condition. He in turn sought out the help of the village leader, who instructed his wife to take Debbie into their home for treatment.

With Debbie in good hands, I accompanied the chief and a dozen natives to a nearby forest to hunt for reptiles. Several of them asked what kind of animals I was looking for, and when they learned that I was mostly interested in finding snakes, they nodded in unison and uttered a Malagasy word, whereupon I was led to a deep, narrow well in the center of the village. Pointing to the well, the chief explained that I would find a snake at the bottom. None of the townspeople came anywhere near the well as they believed it contained some kind of dangerous serpent. Since, as I have said, there are no venomous species of snakes in Madagascar, I climbed down the ladder without hesitation. As the villagers gathered around to watch, silence came over the crowd. When I began my descent into the narrow space, I realized that because the well was so narrow, bending down to examine the area around my feet would be impossible. There was only one way I could accomplish this task: climb down the ladder headfirst. As I lowered myself, I could hear loud murmurs from the gathered masses above. When I reached the bottom rung, I discovered a deep hole in the side of the well that met it at a right angle. Because I was unable to see more than a few inches into the dark hole in my upside-down position, I had to ascend the ladder again for a flashlight. Armed with all the essential equipment, I made my third and final descent. With the blood rushing to my head, I had difficulty seeing clearly into the four-foot-deep hole, although I was able to confirm that nothing was in it. When I made it back to the surface, everyone took several steps back, anticipating my capture of the "demon" snake. I could see the disappointed look on their faces when I showed them my empty pillowcase. Undaunted by this setback, the chief led me to a dead tree where, he said, a large lizard lived high up inside one of its large, hollow branches.

It is one thing to climb a tree as a youth; it is quite another to try it in your late thirties with an entire village watching your every move. With dozens of spectators cheering me on, I managed to climb close to the lizard's lair and to my surprise saw the reptile wedged in the hollow end of the branch. Clutching the tree with one hand, I used my other hand to rock the dead branch from side to side. Soon I heard a loud cracking sound, and seconds later the gecko scrambled out of its hiding place, nearly running right into my hand. With the gecko securely in my grasp, I now had to come down from the tree using only one hand and without either losing the lizard or falling to my death. A minute later, I landed uninjured on the ground, where I was met with spontaneous applause from the onlookers.

In addition to my own efforts, the chief had instructed several of his tribesmen to seek out and capture whatever reptiles they could find. Within two hours, they had brought in several more spiny-tailed iguanas *(Oplurus* sp.), a skink *(Mabuya madagascariensis),* and three small snakes. I thanked the chief for his efforts and returned to his home to check on Debbie's condition. To my surprise, she was sitting up and looking considerably perkier than she had earlier in the morning. She had been given some herbal tea and rice and said that she now felt much better. With that good news, we began our trek northeast towards the center of the country.

The "road" (essentially shallow tracks in the dirt) eventually led us to Isalo National Park. This region, located outside the spiny desert, is more

Isalo National Park showing the main "highway" to the entrance.

Ornate grasshopper
(Phymateus saxsosa)
collected on a
mountaintop in
southwestern
Madagascar.

mountainous than any other region we had visited. The park was created to showcase a natural rock formation at its borders that many believe looks like a mother with her small daughter by her side. (Personally, I think it looks like a woman sitting next to a dog.) At any rate, we were glad to be off the road and setting up camp. As the sun went down, it cast a golden light on the surrounding rocks and open prairie, making the scene look more like the Scottish countryside than the Malagasy highlands.

Exhausted from the drive, we ate dinner and then spent the remainder of the night near our tents, staring up at the cloudless sky and the millions of bright stars. With the refreshingly cool mountain temperatures and with my belly full from a delicious evening meal, I fell asleep in a matter of seconds.

The next morning we set out to climb one of the nearby mountains. It was not particularly large or steep, but to carry all our camera gear and other equipment up the slopes was laborious and time consuming. Just the walk from our vehicle to the foot of the mountain was difficult. Judging from the position of our camp, I estimated that to reach the base would take only about ten minutes. Surprisingly, the trek took two and a half hours.

I was pleased to be in an area where I could again flip rocks to look for animals, but my success here was modest at best. Under a small piece of wood, I found a diurnal dwarf gecko *(Lygodactylus madagascariensis),* and under a rock not much bigger than the animal it sheltered, I caught a granular puddle frog *(Scaphiophryne [Pseudohemisus] granulatus).* On the top of the mountain, I captured an adult Bastard's gecko and the most spectacular insect of the entire trip—a four-inch-long grasshopper (*Phymateus saxosus*) with large red and blue spines all over its body. When it flew, it revealed a crimson red hue under its wings—spectacular.

On the other side of the mountain, Joe and Gary discovered a small waterfall that emptied into a miniature pond. The water was crystal clear and somewhat cold. Walking around this tiny oasis, Joe caught what looked more like a ghost than a species of frog: *Heterixalus tricolor*. It was entirely white except for its feet, which were vivid orange. Altogether, they caught several more frogs, though nothing matched the beauty of their first catch.

On the hike back to the car, we found several more colubrid snakes (*Mimophis mahfalensis*). The open plain (this one was actually a fallow rice paddy) is the favorite haunt of this small serpent.

With only a day remaining before our European companions had to be back in the capital for their flight home, we wasted no time driving back to Tana. In town, we traded addresses with our new friends and wished them a safe journey home. Then we exchanged our large rental vehicle for a smaller, more economical one and finally made our way to the eastern rain forests. Much of the wildlife that typifies Madagascar is found in the dwindling forests of the east, and I was eager to spend a few days searching it out.

Our first stop was the town of Ranomafana (east). This is not to be confused with the town of the same name located several hundred miles to the south. (Actually, there are several villages throughout Madagascar that share this name, which translates to "hot springs.") The southern town of Ranomafana is a protected area managed by North Carolina's Duke University, and collecting wildlife there is strictly prohibited. I emphasize this for clarity, as we did not remove any wildlife from the southern locality. We were initially drawn to the area by the large sign on the side of the road which read simply, "Restaurant." While we waited for our food, a native gentleman showed up behind the restaurant carrying an enormous freshwater "eel." The proprietor took the fish into the kitchen and weighed it before buying it. I watched in disbelief as the scale topped off at ten kilograms (twenty-two pounds). I asked the storeowner if I could take a picture of him holding the eel and he obliged. The "eel," at least four feet long, appeared to have some sort of vestigial "legs" on its back end. Although only three species of eels occur in Madagascar, I have shown the picture of this aquatic animal to a number of ichthyologists, and none has had a clue to its identity.

Local merchant weighing a giant freshwater eel that he has just purchased from a young fisherman in eastern Madagascar.

From our table we could see several small cottages in back of the restaurant. Our guide inquired whether it was possible to rent these rooms, and we were informed that we could, but the cost per night would be a whopping eighty cents. Each eight-foot-square room contained only a small bed; it had neither electricity nor a toilet. Despite these shortcomings, we were pleased to have found this place, for without it we would have had to pitch tents in the forthcoming heavy rains. Immediately outside our rooms was a pristine-looking river surrounded by forests, an ideal place to collect at night.

When darkness fell, we walked along the water's edge, shining our flashlights onto every shrub and tree and finding several species of frogs amidst the riverbank foliage. One of the more stunning species, *Boophis rappiodes,*

A treefrog (*Boophis rapiodes*) found along a river in an eastern rain forest of Madagascar.

was a member of the treefrog family (not Hylidae, like those in North America, but Rhacophoridae). Lime green on the sides and legs, the frog has a bright yellow stripe running from behind each eye back along its flanks to the hind legs. Its back and head have bright red spots, and its eyes are encircled by powder blue rings. In addition, its underside is semitranslucent. We caught several of these exquisite animals, and each time we found one, everyone gathered around it to "ooh and aah." Another species of *Boophis* collected here was the larger *B. difficilis*, a species we nicknamed "the cross-eyed frog," not because it has an ocular problem, but because the frog has a straight line running vertically through its horizontal pupil, giving the impression of a perfect cross. This species is light orange-brown with small, scalloped edges along its limbs. The iris is silvery white with a black ring encircling the entire eye. Adding to its beauty are light blue or green flecks near the black eye ring.

At the site where we did most of our collecting, the stream was only fifteen to twenty feet wide, but we did not test its depth. At a particularly narrow and shallow point in the stream, I glanced up into the dark canopy and saw a thin, spindly twig almost midway between the shores. Near the bottom end of the twig was what I thought to be a shriveled leaf. I called the others over to look at it, knowing they had much better eyesight than I did, and pointed out the tiny, distant object. Everyone shined their flashlights skyward, squinting in an effort to identify this mystery "leaf." Gary, who thought it might be a lizard, made a feeble attempt to climb a nearby tree and shake it loose. I also thought it was a lizard but saw no way to get close to it. After studying the situation for a moment, I tried to knock it down with one of my large rubber bands. I took careful aim then shot my elastic missile at the branch. To my utter surprise, the rubber band hit the branch just above the "leaf," tearing it cleanly from the rest of the tree. A second later, the twig floated gently down and landed on Joe's shoulder. When we saw what it was, we were all speechless. Looking dazed and bewildered, a tiny, two-inch-long chameleon uncurled from its perch and began to explore Joe's neck.

We immediately began an intensive search through the thin, vinelike vegetation to find more of these fascinating and diminutive chameleons. Once we knew where to look, finding them was easy. Joe quickly caught four more, although they were half the size of the first one and none had the small nasal protuberance of the larger specimen. These, we soon discovered, were juveniles. Not long after Joe's haul, I found what I believed to be an adult male, since it had a three-quarter-inch-long, multicolored nasal appendage. It was the most spectacular chameleon I had ever seen. We identified it as a long-nosed dwarf chameleon *(Calumma [Chamaeleo] gallus)*. With an adult length of only two inches, this is one of the smallest chameleons known. Only the diminutive *Brookesia minima* is smaller (and at just over an inch in length, vies for the title of the smallest vertebrate on earth). Just before midnight, when rain began to fall in earnest, we called it quits and retired to our spacious "suites" for the night.

The following morning, under clear blue skies, we resumed our search for wildlife. Near a cluster of thatched-roof huts we found a pile of logs that, when moved, yielded a few common skinks *(Mabuya)* and some gorgeous day geckos *(Phelsuma)*. Most prevalent among the latter genus were the peacock day gecko *(P. quadriocellata)* and the lined day gecko *(P. lineata)*. As I flipped the bottom log, I saw a tiny, black snake trying to

A male long-nosed dwarf chameleon *(Calumma gallus)* found sleeping at night in eastern Madagascar.

burrow into the dirt. This was the familiar, cosmopolitan Brahminy blind snake. A moment later, one of the natives pointed to a pile of dead leaves and said something to us in Malagasy. I knelt down next to the leaf pile and slowly raked through it. Seconds later I uncovered a small colubrid snake resembling a North American garter snake. This two-foot-long adult was *Liopholidophis lateralis.*

Apparently our enthusiasm for snake collecting was a source of entertainment for the locals. A young man in the crowd asked us if we wanted any additional specimens, and we nodded yes in unison. The youth led us to a nearby field, pointed to a distant clump of bamboo, and said he had seen a *do* there a short while ago. The *do* is the local name for the island's boas, in this particular case, the Madagascar tree boa, *Sanzinia madagascariensis.* (Recent taxonomic changes now call it *Boa mandrita,* a name many herpetologists are reluctant to accept.) As Gary approached the bamboo, he suddenly broke into a full run, for he had just seen a boa leave the bamboo and crawl into the thick underbrush. Luckily, he captured the reptile before it could escape. It was a beautiful adult female that, to our surprise, made no attempt to strike or bite. Like the island's tortoises, the three native boa species are protected, so we were obliged to let her go but not before we took photos of each of us holding the snake.

Noting our success with catching the *do,* our native friends were anxious for us to tackle a small problem that was plaguing them. Apparently there was a long-term resident snake in the nearby woods that made some of the locals apprehensive. As we approached the large tree near which the snake had last been seen, one of the natives pointed to the hole at the base of the trunk and said: "*Menarana, menarana!*" This is the local name for the giant hognose snake, *Lioheterodon madagascariensis.* Certain that no dangerously venomous snakes inhabit Madagascar, Gary knelt in front of the tree hole and thrust his hand inside. Immediately we heard a loud, drawn-out hiss. The natives watched in horror as Gary pulled out a striking, hissing four-foot-long snake. Fearful for their safety, the natives scrambled up into the tree. The Malagasy people believe this snake is highly venomous and its bite deadly. Only after Gary secured the snake in a pillowcase did the men come down from the tree.

Back at our rooms, I photographed the day's catch and keyed out the species I could not initially identify. Before leaving the area, I reflected on our productive stay and the beauty of these forests.

• •

We had only a few days left to spend here in the eastern forests, and early the next morning we drove a short distance to the north. We decided to make our last campsite in Madagascar along a small stream in the dense forest. As we had discovered in most third world countries, the local people were quick to find us. With our guides interpreting, I asked the village chief if his people would help us find reptiles and amphibians. The chief was willing to help but needed to know which species we wanted. Preparing for such an eventuality, I had brought a small stack of photos with me to illustrate for the locals some of the indigenous eastern species of reptiles. When I showed the chief a picture of a leaf-tailed gecko (*Uroplatus fimbriatus*), he became animated and repeated the Malagasy name, *"taha-fisaka,"* several times. He was indeed familiar with this lizard but explained that the only way he could catch this species was at the end of his spear. I did not understand what he was trying to tell me, so I asked our guide for an interpretation. It seems that the Malagasy people believe that the adhesive toe pads, which these lizards use to cling to tree trunks, are so powerful that if the gecko lands on a person's body, the only way to remove the lizard is to cut away the victim's skin. Other herps featured in the pictures we showed him were either *fady* to collect or were unfamiliar to him. We thanked him for his assistance and headed off into the forest.

Along a shallow stream, we found several small, nondescript frogs that appeared to be recently metamorphosed. Most were less than half an inch long and unidentifiable. Under some fallen tree limbs, I caught a pair of Malagasy giant pill millipedes (genus *Sphaerotherium*), which, like the ones in the United States, roll up into a ball when molested. Here, however, they were metallic green and when rolled up were the size of golf balls.

As the sun disappeared, we started back to camp. Fortunately we had our flashlights with us, allowing us to continue herping in the dark. Gary suddenly stopped and focused his light to the side of the trail.

"What's up?" I asked him.

"Snake!" he responded, and quickly ran off the road to capture it. He returned to show us a somber-looking serpent, all grayish black, with no pattern.

"What is it?" Joe asked.

"Beats me," I replied. I was not aware of any all black snakes that lived there. We tried to key it out over dinner but were unsuccessful.

We spent an additional day in the rain forest and then headed back to Tana, where we checked into our old hotel. My first stop was the permit office. After years of negotiations with foreign permit offices, I had come to expect complications, and again I was not disappointed. The permit official informed me that my permits would not be ready for at least two weeks, and I quickly explained to him that I would be leaving Madagascar in three days. He apologized for this inconvenience but said that no permits could be issued until we had fully complied with all the terms and conditions of the permit. I asked him what terms I had failed to comply with and he said that first, I had failed to have a Malagasy student accompany us into the field. He stated that, in addition, I was to have purchased a vehicle that would be left behind for their use, donated a percentage of the preserved wildlife to the local university, left all my collecting equipment and field guides with their office, and, finally, I was to have taken two Malagasy students back with me to the United States for one year, so they could be trained in wildlife collection and specimen preservation.

That's all? I explained to this gentleman that at no time were any of the aforementioned conditions revealed to me, and that as an individual, I could not afford so great a financial burden. He said that I was not an "individual," since I was supported by a zoo, a university, and a museum.

We did ultimately reach an agreement: I was to leave behind all my field equipment (tent, sleeping bag, dissecting kit, books, etc.) as well as some of the preserved specimens. This I thought was a more reasonable request, and after agreeing to these conditions, I was finally granted an export permit. One catch, however, was that the permit might not be ready before my departure. The officials assured me they would do everything possible to expedite the documents but warned that I might have to delay my departure. This was not possible, as my airline tickets could not be changed. Our guide, Philippe, promised to ship the animals to me in the event the permits were not ready in time. It was a nice gesture, and it took some of the pressure off the situation.

My next stop was at Dr. Domergue's office to ask for his help in identifying the few species we had been unable to name. (This was necessary in order to obtain an accurate export permit.) When I showed Dr. Domergue the grayish black snake that Gary had caught, his eyes grew wide with excitement. He explained that he believed this was probably a member of the colubrid genus *Pseudoxyrhopus*, but it was definitely a species he had never seen before, and it might be new to science. Gary was thrilled to hear this as he was hoping that the snake might be named after him (*P. "miguesi"*). Dr. Domergue asked if he could keep the snake overnight to try to identify it positively. We left all the live specimens behind and promised we would return in the morning to take care of them.

When we returned the next morning, Dr. Domergue looked exhausted. Staying up most of the night trying to key out our mystery snake, he had made detailed drawings of the serpent's head, tail, body scalation, and even its dentition. His declaration was that it was a *Pseudoxyrhopus*, but not a new species. He said it was *P. microps*, an obscure snake known from only a single specimen. After returning to the States, I found that there have actually been seven or eight known specimens of this species.

It was good timing that brought us back to the capital on Friday, as it gave us one last chance to walk through the *zoma* and finish our gift shopping. Although low on funds, we still had several rolls of U.S. toilet paper and figured we could use them to make some great deals. Also, even though most of our clothes were in bad shape, many of the vendors were eager to swap local handicrafts for them.

We ended up with some nice souveniers: wood carvings of chameleons, exotic musical instruments, jewelry, and colorful textiles. Our hope now was that we could stuff them all into our luggage for the long trip home.

The following day brought no further news regarding export permits. With only one day left before our departure, I was becoming extremely anxious, but after spending most of the day at Dr. Domergue's facility taking care of the reptiles and amphibians, we were ready to go out on the town to forget our problems and celebrate our last day in Madagascar.

Departure Day. It was now obvious that the permits would not be forthcoming, so I asked Philippe if he would make good on his promise and ship the animals to me as soon as the permits were ready. He said he would check on the permit status daily until they became available then send the specimens to me by priority air express. Despite the somewhat sour ending to our trip, we had had a fantastic time in Madagascar. As if to wish us a *bon voyage,* a beautiful rainbow appeared over Tana as we boarded the taxi to the airport. I took my last photo of the city, and we were homeward bound.

While waiting to board our "time machine" to take us back to the present, I could not help but reflect on an appropriate Malagasy proverb that I had recently learned: *"Behave like a chameleon; keep one eye on the future, but always observe the past."*

••

As soon as I returned to the United States, I telephoned Philippe to determine what progress had been made toward the permit acquisition. (It had taken us nearly two days to fly back.) Philippe informed me that there were further complications, and that if I wanted the permits, I would have to pay another fee. I had known that as soon as I left Madagascar, the authorities would give me the runaround. I asked how much this was going to cost me, and Philippe said, "Five hundred U.S. dollars." Great. Not only had I just spent several thousand dollars to make this trip, but now I had to shell out an additional five hundred dollars. I was furious, but I realized there was nothing I could do. If I declined to pay the fee, all the hard work we had endured would be for nothing. I told Philippe that I would send the money the next morning. He said that he would go ahead and pay the fee for me, and then I in turn should send him the money. I agreed, and the next morning his money was on its way.

The story, however, does not end here; there were more complications ahead. Despite my daily phone calls to Philippe over the next five days, the permits were still not forthcoming. Incidentally, Madagascar is the only country (at least at that time) to which one cannot dial direct; instead, you must involve a local operator at a cost of four dollars per minute. After ten more days of waiting, I received a collect call at 3:30 A.M. from Air France in Paris informing me that a large box from Madagascar was at their facility. The gentleman then explained that the box (cardboard, with Styrofoam inside) could not be shipped as is, but instead had to be constructed of wood. He then offered to have one made for me—at a cost of $550, including shipping. Again, I did not have much choice, so I gave him my credit card number and authorized him to proceed.

When I arrived at the airport the following morning to pick up the shipment, I faced still more complications. When Air France placed the original box into the wooden one, they failed to list the contents on the outside of the new crate, as required by law. The local U.S. Fish and Wildlife agent informed me that this was a serious violation, and that she could confiscate the entire shipment. Further, there was a foul smell coming from the crate, indicating that some of the animals were dead. She added that the shipment could be confiscated if there were "excessive" numbers of dead animals. I asked her what the definition of "excessive" was, and she said that it was her call to make that determination.

Unfortunately, there were some dead animals, but only a relative few. The agent finally cleared the shipment, and I was free to leave. The entire episode was extremely stressful but in the end well worth the effort.

••

A year after the trip, with several of my parasitology colleagues, I coauthored an article that was published. In that scientific paper, we named seven new species of microscopic parasites that had come from various Malagasy lizards and snakes. I named one of them after my field assistant and friend, Joe Furman, for all his hard work and dedication in the field over the last few years. When I finally showed him the article, he was ecstatic to be honored in that way. For the next week, he carried the article with him and showed it to anyone and everyone who would listen. And, while the naming of the parasite was certainly intended as praise, I could not help but taunt Joe occasionally, saying, "Don't get so excited. After all, I named something that came out of a lizard's butt after you." He did not care; he was thrilled.

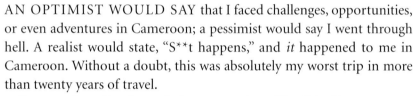

CHAPTER 7

The Snake Men of Cameroon

AN OPTIMIST WOULD SAY that I faced challenges, opportunities, or even adventures in Cameroon; a pessimist would say I went through hell. A realist would state, "S**t happens," and *it* happened to me in Cameroon. Without a doubt, this was absolutely my worst trip in more than twenty years of travel.

Just two days after the end of my 1990 trip to Namibia, I began preparations to visit Cameroon. Due to the large number of endemic reptiles and amphibians in Cameroon and the fact that little had been done there in terms of herpetological parasitology, I considered this an ideal place to continue my research. I began by contacting the Cameroon Embassy in the United States, requesting names and telephone numbers of wildlife permit authorities in Cameroon. When I was given the name of the appropriate official, I made several calls to the Cameroonian capital of Youande. Each time I was told that the research director was in a meeting and could not come to the telephone. I tried to leave my name with the receptionist so she could advise the director of my wish to conduct research in Cameroon, but each call ended the same way.

"Hello, this is Paul Freed calling from the United States. I would like to speak to the Director of Wildlife Research please."

"Could you please spell your last name?"

"F-R-E-E . . .," and before I could say "D," I heard the sound of the telephone disconnecting, then a dial tone. I immediately called back and had a repeat of the same scenario. I tried this three times, but nothing changed. Since Cameroon is seven hours ahead of Central Standard Time, I had to get up very early in the morning to make the calls, so at this point I was utterly exasperated.

A few days later I telephoned my friend, Stephanie, in Pennsylvania who teaches French and asked her if she would call the Cameroon permit office on my behalf and explain to the receptionist what I was attempting to do. I warned her what had transpired between the receptionist and me and suggested that if she spoke in French, the country's primary language, she might have more success. When Stephanie called me back the next day, she too was extremely irritated. She explained that she had just engaged in one of the most infuriating telephone conversations of her life. Each time she had tried to convey my intentions, the voice at the other end would interrupt and ask for the spelling of my last name. Each time Stephanie got to the letter "D" in my last name, the woman hung up. This happened three times. Stephanie finally determined that to successfully reach the permit office, I would need to send them a certified letter by air courier. With my research proposal completed, I sent the first of four letters to the permit office by courier, each of which cost sixty-seven dollars to mail.

Eleven and a half months later, just three days before our intended departure, I still had no permit. With airline tickets in hand and time off from work already approved, I decided to go ahead with the trip anyway.

As on other recent trips, I was accompanied on this expedition by Debbie and Joe but not, this time, by Gary. Another herp enthusiast, Mike, replaced him. Debbie and Joe had been with me on several other international trips but this was Mike's first trip with us. Little did we know that he had chosen a terrible time to join us.

• •

We arrived at the city of Douala in the southwestern region of the country just before midnight. As the plane door opened, a wall of hot, humid air greeted us. As Houstonians, we were used to high humidity, but the sticky, fetid wave that assaulted us was almost more than we could bear. The temperature was easily in the upper nineties and the humidity was even higher.

We waited by the baggage claim area with anticipation, hoping that all our belongings would arrive safely. As a sign of bad things to come, two pieces of luggage that contained the bulk of our research equipment did not arrive. Gone were a microscope, a battery-operated centrifuge, all the preserving equipment, and much more.

We hailed a cab to find a hotel in which to spend the night. When the taxi driver saw our mountain of luggage, he said that we would need a second vehicle to transport our belongings. Moments later another taxi arrived, and we were taken to a nearby hotel. After unloading our things, the taxi drivers impatiently demanded their money. Having no local currency, we tried a ploy that worked for us in Madagascar: instead of cash, we gave the drivers tee shirts, chocolate, and batteries. However, they threw the items to the ground, then in loud, irritated voices again demanded payment in local currency. The hotel manager who witnessed our dilemma stepped in and paid the two men, explaining that he would simply add the cab fare to our bill. In the hour we had been in the country, we had interacted with four or five locals, each of whom had been rude and arrogant. We had no idea that they would be among the friendlier people we would encounter on our monthlong expedition.

We were finally led up three flights of stairs to our humble, overpriced rooms (fifty-five dollars for a tiny, squalid box with no bathroom, one towel, and no bed sheets). It was past 1:00 A.M., and after more than twenty hours with virtually no sleep, we turned in for the night.

At 7:00 A.M. the next day, I telephoned the airport and learned that our bags had continued south to the country of Gabon where, I was told, they would be placed on the next available flight and returned to us later that afternoon. As we stumbled around town looking for a bank to convert our dollars to Cameroon francs, a young man approached and asked whether we needed help. When we explained our dilemma, he escorted us to a bank and helped us with all the complicated forms necessary to accomplish our goal. This simple task took a monumental two hours. There were no structured lines anywhere; people just pushed and shoved, then waved their money at a teller in hopes of being next. I finally caught on to their technique, and minutes later I had exchanged our money. When it was over, we never wanted to set foot in another bank, but unfortunately, we were forced to go through this nightmare several more times during our stay.

Now our goal was to rent a vehicle and drive to the permit office as soon as possible. The hotel lobby had a few advertisements for car rental agencies, and after getting directions, we walked the mile or so to the nearest one. The walk provided an opportunity for us to see some of the city and its inhabitants. We were surprised by the trash and filth that littered the streets. These conditions attracted flies that in turn caught the attention of the agama lizards that lived in the trash. These agamas (*Agama agama*) were plentiful and like some other lizard species were sexually dimorphic—males have a red head and a dark blue black body; females are uniformly brown.

To our surprise, the rental agency people were actually friendly and eager to do business with us, but when we discovered their exorbitant rental rates, we understood the reason for their hospitality. For a large vehicle that would comfortably accommodate all of our possessions and us, the fee was three thousand dollars for three weeks. This did not include the mileage fee, which would add an additional forty-five cents per mile. After checking two other car rental agencies, we discovered that the first one was the cheapest of the three. Despite splitting the bill four ways, we were going to seriously compromise our financial situation. But we had little choice in the matter, so we reluctantly returned to the original agency.

With Joe nervously behind the wheel of our new four-wheel-drive vehicle, we were on our way to the American Embassy to check in and to ask for directions to the permit office.

Here, in the southwestern region of the country, the main language is French. In the central and eastern regions, English is more commonly used, although we soon learned that throughout Cameroon several hundred dialects are spoken. Consequently, we would need to hire a guide who could communicate with more than just one indigenous tribe.

The drive from the rental agency to the American Embassy was short. As we approached the building, we saw an American flag waving in the hot, gentle breeze. We felt a great sense of pride at being Americans until I noticed a sign in French right outside the compound doors that read, *"Defense d'uriner ici"* (do not piss here). This was not my idea of a friendly welcome but was either indicative of toilet habits of the locals or perhaps their feelings about Americans.

We parked the vehicle close to the sign and went inside, where we were greeted by warm, friendly smiles of U.S. officials. One of them agreed that it was prudent to make our presence known to the Embassy, as there had been several recent altercations between Americans and local people. He made copies of our passports and suggested we show only the duplicates to officials requesting them. We asked him to help us find a guide to take us around the country. He made a phone call, and within minutes a young man appeared at the door. He was Denis Achu, a polite, soft-spoken young

A sign in French at the American Embassy (building on far left) in Douala, Cameroon, advises passersby "Do Not Piss Here."

man who could not have been more than twenty years old. Although he was familiar with several regional dialects, he had never been in the "bush." We thanked the Embassy personnel for all their courtesies, then made our way to the permit office across town.

Our drive along the busy thoroughfares took us past magnificent statues, old buildings, and, in general, great views of the city and its people. With my camera around my neck, I took pictures of everything and everyone I saw. When Denis noticed what I was doing, he became quite agitated and advised me to stop photographing at once. When I asked why, he said that there was a strict prohibition against taking pictures of government buildings, military personnel, policemen, statues, streets where parades have been held, and closely related objects and locations. I soon found that photo restrictions were not limited to just those subjects. While driving along a side street, we became lost and eventually pulled up beside a woman sitting in her front yard to ask for directions. As Denis talked to the woman, a beautiful adult male agama appeared from behind a tree. The lizard was about fifteen feet away from the woman, and when I raised my camera to photograph it, the woman screamed that I could not take her picture. When I tried to explain that I was photographing the lizard and not her, she screamed even louder. Denis advised me to put the camera away and not photograph anything else in the city.

I could see I was going to have problems here, since in addition to herpetology, one of my main interests is photography. But, as they say, "Necessity is the mother of invention," so I soon "invented" several new ways to take pictures. One technique was what I called "hip" photography. With the camera slung over my shoulder and hanging harmlessly at my hip, I estimated the approximate distance to my subject then distracted onlookers by pointing to an imaginary object in the other direction. With everyone looking the other way, I carefully depressed the shutter button and, voila, with some luck captured the desired image. A second technique I used when I was close to someone I wanted to photograph was what I called "sneeze" photography. At the moment I depressed the shutter release button, I produced a loud, fake sneeze that masked the sound of the camera. My last method I termed "machine-gun photography." This involved the use of a power-winder attached to the camera, which I pointed out of the vehicle window. With a single touch of the shutter release, I was able to take a rapid series of ten to twenty photographs in just a few seconds, hoping that one of the images would turn out well. Although these techniques may seem half-baked and preposterous to a "real" photographer, they did allow me to get photographs I otherwise would have missed.

When the irate woman finally gave us directions, we were again on our way to the permit office. At a nearby intersection, a policeman stood in the middle of the road directing traffic. We needed to take a left turn here, and after he motioned for us to proceed with the turn, the officer suddenly blew his whistle and put up his hand, stopping us in our tracks. Apparently, in Cameroon you do not turn in *front* of the policeman; instead, you go behind him. The officer stopped all traffic in the intersection and came over to our vehicle. Seeing that we were tourists, he asked Joe for his passport. Forgetting the advice the U.S. Embassy had given us just minutes earlier, Joe handed over his original passport, rather than the copy. The policeman instructed Joe to pull the car off to the side of the road then strode back into the intersection and continued to direct traffic. Now what?

We all sat in silence for a few minutes until Denis finally spoke up and said he would have a talk with the cop and try to resolve this problem. For what seemed like hours, Denis and the policeman spoke in the intersection, each making many exaggerated hand gestures. Finally, Denis walked back to the car and in so many words asked Joe for some cash to bribe the officer.

"How much should I offer?" Joe asked meekly.

"Give me fifty dollars and I'll see what I can do," Denis responded. Armed with Joe's money, he again huddled with the cop, who quickly abandoned his post in the middle of the street and walked to the more discrete cover of a nearby bus stop. Denis shook the policeman's hand, and in a few seconds we were on our way again. Joe was so relieved at not going to jail that he did not care about the money. We later related this incident to the staff at the American Embassy, and they all laughed, asking whether we had killed the president. They said that you could literally bribe your way out of a murder charge for less than twenty dollars. This was good to know, since it would not be the last time we would be detained by the police in Cameroon.

At the permit office, we found the official in charge of scientific research. He pulled out a file with my name on it and to my surprise, it had the four sixty-seven-dollar letters inside. After briefly introducing myself and describing to him my research needs, I nervously asked the question I dread at each of these interviews, "How many specimens of each species may I collect?" His answer surprised and shocked me.

"How much money do you have?" he asked.

"I'm sorry, I don't understand," I said. "I'm not interested in a commercial permit, just a scientific one."

"Yes, this is for a scientific permit," he went on to explain, "and the cost of just the permit is four hundred dollars. If you wish a commercial permit, that will cost you one thousand dollars."

I was horrified. At no time during our previous communications was there any mention of a permit fee. Yet that was only the beginning. When I asked how many specimens of each species I would be allowed to collect with a permit, he pulled out two pieces of paper and asked again, "How much money do you have?"

Now I was completely overwhelmed. Listed on the two sheets of paper were essentially all the major species of wildlife known to occur in Cameroon. Although the list was in French, I was able to read most of it and was flabbergasted by what I saw. In addition to reptile and amphibian rosters, there were extensive lists of birds, mammals, and even insects! And despite the fact that Cameroon is considered a signatory of CITES (Convention on International Trade in Endangered Species), protected and endangered species of animals were included for sale on this list. For twenty-four hundred dollars you could export a gorilla; for eight hundred dollars, a young chimpanzee. And if you could afford the shipping costs, you could buy an elephant or hippopotamus. On the herpetological side of the "menu," crocodiles and sea turtles—both Appendix I (endangered) on the CITES list—could be collected and exported. Most herps averaged between five and twenty dollars each. Even the Goliath frog (*Conraua goliath*), the largest frog on earth, could be obtained for eight dollars a specimen. If insects were to your liking, you could have them for two dollars apiece. Thus, if you had the money, essentially any living creature in the country was available. After returning to the United States, I showed the lists to many people, and all were astonished. I understand that since my visit to Cameroon, some of these policies have changed.

What we learned from wildlife officials was completely disconcerting; the policy meant a radically different approach to specimen collecting and a reduction in the number of animals we could afford to export back to the States. It meant that in the field we would need to empty our collecting bags at the end of each day then count our money to determine which animals we could afford to keep. Since we had come this far and had already spent a small fortune on plane tickets, equipment, and the rental car, we reluctantly accepted the conditions of the permit office.

Another minor setback was having to declare beforehand in which provinces we wished to collect. When I questioned this requirement, the wildlife official clarified it by saying that if we were found in a region for which we did not have a permit, we would be jailed. Realizing that under these circumstances we would be unable to cover much territory in the country during the next three weeks, we opted to visit just the western and southwestern regions. With the required documents now in our possession, we thanked the permit officer and explained that we would return several days before our departure date and submit a list of all the animals collected.

Before leaving town, we stopped at Denis's home to pick up some of his belongings. He lived in a modest neighborhood, where most houses had no electricity or running water and where the majority of homes (his included) had dirt floors. As we drove through the maze of shanty dwellings, Denis instructed me where and when to turn. Since none of the narrow roads had street signs, he described landmarks at which I needed to turn. As we approached one particular intersection, he told me to turn left. Since there were two streets very close to one another, I asked him, "Which street?"

"There. Right there. Take a left at the duck," he said. We laughed for days afterwards at his overall innocence and gentle ways.

We loaded Denis's things into the car and began our trek north of Douala to rain forests near the town of Nkongsamba. As we drove through several towns, I noticed tables set up along roadsides, each with giant glass jars on them. At first I thought they contained local "moonshine" or perhaps some type of honey or molasses, but Denis explained that they contained gasoline. When we stopped to examine one of them closely, I could hardly believe that people actually stored gas this way; most of the containers had a large amount of debris on the bottom, and even more junk floated on top. Denis told us that when you purchase gas from these vendors, they first pour it through a piece of cloth to filter out the impurities. He also stated that all of this roadside gas comes from neighboring Nigeria, where it sells for less than half of what gas stations charge in Cameroon. I was determined not to put it in our vehicle.

Since it was sundown when we arrived at the small village of Nkongsamba, we decided to stay in a hotel rather than search for a camping area in the dark. As Denis negotiated our stay at the "Hotel Happy," we waited outside this two-star resort and listened to the mice and rats scurrying around the dirt floor at the entrance to the lobby. The best deal Denis could make was to get two rooms for the exorbitant rate of forty dollars each. In return, we got a "bed" (again, with no sheets), a wash basin (no running water), and a communal "toilet" (a hole in the floor in the corner of a doorless room). It did not take long to realize that Cameroon was not an AAA-recommended tourist destination.

Following a terrible night's sleep (thanks to bugs, rodents, and heat), I awoke early the next morning to hear Joe's screams coming from the bathroom next door. With no running water in the hotel, Joe was forced to bathe by pouring a bucket of cold rainwater over his head.

Following a quick breakfast (elsewhere), we continued our search for pristine forest, and by early afternoon we had located a suitable camping area far from any town or people—or so we thought. Just as we finished clearing the brush and setting up our tents, we were inundated by natives who regularly wandered through our "private" compound. Although they were humble and polite, we were still uncomfortable with the idea that while we were out collecting animals, they would have access to our belongings. We remedied this by ensuring that one of us was always in camp.

Heat and humidity here were brutal. Adding to the discomfort were hordes of pesky mosquitoes and swarms of tiny, biting black flies. We later learned that these flies carry the parasite that causes African sleeping sickness. Despite the liberal use of insect repellents, Debbie eventually was covered with hundreds of large welts on her arms and legs. At night she lay awake in the tent, scratching herself raw, and in two days she had a bad infection. Although not affected as seriously as Debbie, the guys were very uncomfortable being here, so much so that by the end of the second day, they approached me and asked if we could leave early. "Leave the area?" I asked, surprised by their request.

"No," was their response, "we were thinking of leaving the country." Apparently they were fed up with the negative attitude of locals as well as the harsh conditions we had encountered so far.

"Guys, come on, we've been planning this trip for a year and already spent a fortune to get here. If we go back now, it will cost us an arm and a leg to alter our plane tickets," I said, irritated by their change of heart. Instead of leaving, I suggested we try to find a more hospitable habitat.

Denis agreed and said he would ask some locals where we might find a more comfortable area. Within minutes, an elderly man came by, spoke with Denis, then instructed us to follow him. After walking less than a mile, we encountered a large, cool, fast-flowing stream with rocks along the banks that formed shallow ponds. We promptly stripped down to our shorts and dove in. The water was so refreshing that everyone soon forgot about his or her petty problems, and there was no more talk of returning home.

Later that afternoon, we returned to the stream to hunt for frogs, lizards, and snakes. As we busied ourselves flipping over logs and stones, a young man walked by carrying what looked like a rifle from the 1800s. Slung over his shoulder was a freshly killed greater spot-nosed guenon (*Ceropithecus nictitans*) that he had shot after trailing the monkey through the dense forest. When he asked what we were looking for, Denis explained that we were here to collect reptiles and amphibians. A short time later the youth returned and handed Denis a plastic bag. Inside was a live, juvenile white-bellied pangolin *(Manis tricuspis),* a kind of scaly anteater, which the young man apparently believed was a reptile because of its large scales. Although we were excited to see this unusual mammal, we certainly had no use for it; so we photographed it and then started to release it in the nearby woods. But the hunter had different plans for the pangolin. If we did not purchase the animal, it would become his dinner that evening. Because we could not allow such a magnificent animal to be eaten by the young hunter, we paid a few dollars for it with the intention of releasing it later that evening away from prying eyes. But we became so captivated by this gentle, endearing animal that we decided to keep it for another day—until we were sure it was not injured and could fend for itself.

While we searched for herps during the day, we carried the pangolin with us. It stayed hooked onto our belts with its long claws, and when we found an ant nest, we set it down next to the insect colony and watched as it used its long, sticky tongue to lap up the endless stream of ants that boiled out of the burrow. Perhaps because it superficially resembled cer-

A juvenile white-bellied pangolin (*Manis tricuspis*) that was brought to our camp in south-western Cameroon by a local hunter.

tain reptiles or because it was young and cute, we became attached to it and gave serious thought to bringing it back to the States. (According to the permit office, pangolins cost only forty dollars each to export.) However, once back in the United States, the animal would have to undergo an extremely lengthy and expensive quarantine protocol. We decided that the best thing was to release it back into the wild where it belonged.

That evening, the same young man stopped by our campsite and asked if we were interested in collecting any "giant" frogs. We knew that he was referring to the Goliath frog, the largest species of frog on earth. Some specimens of this spectacular amphibian can reach lengths of over twelve inches, and with the hind legs stretched out, they can exceed a total length of twenty-four inches. Although I was anxious to photograph one, I did

The largest species of frog on earth, the Goliath frog *(Conraua goliath)*, collected in south-western Cameroon.

not plan to collect any for export back to the United States, primarily because Cameroon's foremost authority on frogs, Dr. Jean-Louis Amiet, whom we had met in the capital, specifically asked us not to collect and export this amphibian. This request was based on a survey conducted by Dr. Amiet during the previous few years. He had found that populations of Goliath frogs were declining due to excessive collection by locals, who use the frogs as a major food source. He also stated that an animal dealer in the northwestern United States had been illegally exporting large numbers of the frogs, most of which died within a few days of capture.

After dinner we followed the guide and three of his friends several miles into the forest. Eventually, we came upon a large pond in a clearing, where one of the men instructed us to walk quietly and very slowly around the pond's perimeter and shine our flashlights near the water's edge. Within a few minutes we spotted our first giant frog, but I was somewhat disappointed by the animal's unexpectedly small size. Although it was over eight inches long, I had anticipated catching monsters larger than a football. The guides also cautioned us to be on the lookout for venomous water cobras *(Boulengerina annulata)* and black forest cobras *(Naja melanoleuca)*, both of which they said were common in the area. Despite my high hopes of encountering these snakes, the only dangerous animal we saw was a colony of large, biting red ants that invaded Joe's legs and bit him repeatedly.

By evening's end, we had caught three average-sized Goliath frogs, which we eventually released without the natives' knowledge, since they would have kept them for the dinner pot.

The next morning brought even higher temperatures and more biting insects to our campsite; it was time to leave this place and find a more hospitable area. Although Denis had virtually no field experience in his own country, he suggested we collect at the cooler, higher elevations of Mount Cameroon, the highest mountain in the country (forty-one hundred meters), located in the southwestern region near the town of Buea.

The drive along National Route 5 to Buea took several hours. On the way, we passed through numerous small villages, and in each one we saw little shanty huts at which different species of wildlife were being offered for sale. Hanging from wooden poles were a variety of dead monkeys (all protected or endangered species), dwarf species of deer (duikers), brush-tailed porcupines *(Atherurus africanus)*, and even large savanna monitors *(Varanus exanthematicus)*.

Dead monkeys for sale by a roadside in Cameroon.

One man stood by the road holding a large, dead rodent by its tail. As we pulled over and approached him, I asked Denis what kind of animal he was holding, to which Denis replied, "Cutting grass."

"No, I don't care what he does for a living," I said. "What kind of animal is he holding?"

Denis laughed and repeated, "Cutting grass." That was the local name for this animal. I asked the vendor if I could examine it closely.

"Yes, ten dollars," was his reply.

"No, I don't want to buy the animal, I just want to look at it," I said. Again, the man repeated his request for money. Denis then spoke with him in his native language and a deal was struck. For one dollar, I could photograph the man holding the animal. Zooming in with my camera lens, I could now clearly see that he was holding a giant cane rat *(Thryonomys gregorianus)*, a common local rodent that many of the natives like to eat. As we drove away, I asked Denis how long the man would stand there trying to sell his rat. "As long as it takes," Denis said.

"But if no one buys it after a day or two, won't it spoil?" I asked.

"If no one buys it, then he will take it into the nearest village to sell. And if they won't buy it, he will eventually eat it himself," Denis replied.

A short distance from the "rat man," another roadside vendor was holding a four-foot-long, dead savanna monitor. The lizard had a huge gash across its back, indicating that it had been dispatched with a machete. Again, we pulled over and asked if we could photograph the man holding the animal. "Twenty-five dollars," was his response. Denis explained that we did not wish to purchase the animal but merely take a picture of it. His reply did not change. I asked Denis why the local people were so unreasonable concerning the taking of photographs. He explained that several years ago a Frenchman came to Cameroon and took thousands of photographs all across the country then returned to France and published a book of the people and sights he had seen. Supposedly, he made a small fortune from this endeavor and never gave a penny to the people of Cameroon for their help. Now, whenever someone wants to take a picture of a native or wildlife, the locals want their share in advance. As annoying as it was to hear this, it was nonetheless a reasonable explanation.

As we climbed the slopes of Cameroon's highest peak, we could feel the dramatic change in temperature with every kilometer we drove. Halfway up the mountain, at an elevation of approximately two thousand meters, we found a small Presbyterian church with rooms for rent. We went inside to see what was available and discovered a notice posted on a

A native man
in southwestern
Cameroon holding
a "cutting grass,"
a giant cane rat
(*Thryonomys
gregorianus*),
for sale by the
roadside.

wall outside the main office outlining ten rules and conditions regarding room rentals. When I read rule number eight, I had to laugh out loud: "Guests should not *stool* carelessly around the compound." It seemed a necessary warning, given that many of the native men seem quite comfortable relieving themselves in public anywhere and anytime they please. It was not unusual to see men turn their backs on onlookers along the street and urinate whenever the need arose.

We were fortunate to rent two rooms at a reasonable rate, and after unloading the vehicle, we took a much-needed lunch break. Assessing our finances, we realized that since we were beginning to run low on cash, it would be prudent to purchase food at a market instead of eating out, as we had done since the beginning of the journey. Once we stocked up on

Male mountain chameleon (*Chamaeleo montium*) collected in Buea, western Cameroon.

food, we consulted a local map to determine where we should begin collecting. A nice tract of pristine forest was about an hour's hike away, so we gathered our equipment and headed to the woods.

The daytime temperature here averaged a cool seventy degrees, a pleasant change from the oppressive conditions we had endured earlier. At sunset, the temperature dropped considerably, and I was afraid we would find no reptiles or amphibians because of the cold. My fears were alleviated when Mike called out that he had just found a chameleon sleeping on a tree branch about ten feet off the ground. We raced over to see which species he found and quickly identified it as a male mountain chameleon (*Chamaeleo montium*). Of the dozen or so chameleon species known to occur in Cameroon, this is certainly one of the more attractive ones. Males have three long horns protruding from their heads, and their backs and tails are adorned with large, sail-like fins. Their overall coloration is green with numerous lime green and blue spots scattered over the sides of their bodies. Uniformly green females lack horns and high caudal fins. Although we caught only one chameleon on our first day, at least we were in an area where they occurred.

The next day we returned to search for more. Looking for chameleons during the day is like trying to catch fish without a hook. Given their ability to blend in with their surroundings, they are almost impossible to find during the day. A small group of children, attracted by our activities, asked what we were doing. Denis explained that we were trying to find chameleons, to which one of the children immediately responded by pointing to a nearby tree and asking, "You mean like that one?" Sure enough, he had spotted an adult male about twenty feet up in a nearby tree.

"Great," I said, "how are we ever going to get it out of the tree?" The young boys immediately broke off several long, slender branches, and while one of them gently prodded the chameleon from the rear, another boy placed his branch in front of the lizard. The chameleon crept onto the second branch, and the youth then lowered the reptile into my waiting hands. They made it look so easy, and despite all my experience in the field, I doubt that I could have been as successful. We rewarded the children with some sweets, and they happily returned to their previous activities.

In the forest, we walked along a narrow path that eventually led us to two teenage boys who were returning to Buea. Each carried a rifle longer than himself, and each had a different species of monkey he had recently

Two youths show off their prize of "bushmeat" after spending the night in the forest of western Cameroon.

killed. Without thinking or asking permission, I took a picture of both of them, and to my surprise, they did not ask for money or protest what I was doing.

Before nightfall, we returned to our rooms to process the data from the animals collected and to determine which ones we would keep and which we would release. With our money dwindling rapidly, we kept only a few specimens and released the others. Perhaps it was the cooler temperatures or maybe the higher elevation, but so far this region had produced little of interest, other than chameleons. We decided to spend one more day here.

The following morning as we were loading our vehicle, we were drawn to the long hedge of hibiscus in front of the church, only a few feet away. I was initially attracted to an ornate bug that was feeding on one of the flowers when I noticed a juvenile mountain chameleon next to it. A quick search through the rest of the low hedge proved extremely productive; we found fifteen additional specimens. In addition to five more juveniles, we located several adult males and females. And to think that earlier we had trekked for hours just to find a single animal when all along they were abundant right under our noses. Despite our good fortune, we kept only two pairs of adults; we could not afford to keep them all, and we did not want to deplete the local population.

We were reluctant to leave this cool, refreshing, and beautiful place because we knew our next stop would be hot, humid, and miserable. Before leaving town, we filled our gas tank at a local station. Not only were the animals expensive, but the cost of gasoline was almost bankrupting us. Since regular gasoline cost more than $4.50 a gallon, it was no wonder that many people bought their gas from roadside vendors at about half the price. We were rapidly facing the reality that we, too, would soon buy our gasoline from these "glass-jar" vendors.

Next to the gas station an elderly woman sat beside a giant iron pot suspended over a large fire. As she poured a thick liquid into the pot, Denis walked over to her, offered her a few coins, then returned to the car with a small bag of meatball-like food. He offered us each a taste, and our reactions were all the same: we loved them.

"They are just fried dough balls," Denis explained.

"Yes, but they're delicious," we all replied.

"Are they expensive?" I asked. When Denis said that they were about a penny apiece, I leaped from the car and purchased a dollar's worth. It took the woman a few minutes to make that many, but the wait was definitely worthwhile. We left town with both the gas tank and our bellies full. Denis was amused at our reaction to the dough balls; he said that everyone in Cameroon eats them, and they can be purchased on almost every street corner. Cholesterol levels notwithstanding, we now had a cheap food source for the remainder of our stay.

Our next destination was the coastal town of Limbé; however, we had barely made it out of Buea when, once again, we were stopped by a policeman. This time we knew the routine, having now been detained many times before by the local authorities. These stops were not the result of any suspected illegal activities on our part; they were merely opportunities for the cops to make a few bucks. This particular "arrest," I believe, was due to my having two consecutive vowels in my last name. Denis made a futile attempt to talk our way out of the "fine," but the outcome was always the same: pay up or go to jail. Naturally, we always ended up paying the officer to avoid what surely would have been a fate worse than death, a Cameroonian jail. On at least three separate occasions, we were led off to a local jail, where we were threatened with incarceration if we did not pay.

This corruption is not reserved for tourists alone; even locals have to put up with corrupt cops on the take. Locally, police are referred to in French as *mange mille*, translating literally as "eat a thousand" (the local currency, which is equivalent to four U.S. dollars). Buses and taxis stopped by the police also must pay before they can proceed. As a consequence, each passenger has to pay what amounts to a double fee to ride public transportation, one for the fare and the other for the "un-fair." I have watched taxis and buses enter an intersection where a cop was standing, only to have the driver extend his arm out the window and hand the policeman a wad of money without even coming to a full stop.

On one occasion as I was taking video footage on the outskirts of a small town, a man ran towards us, screaming at the top of his voice for a policeman. Apparently, during my filming, I had taken some footage with a Cameroon flag in the distance. In seconds, a policeman showed up and ordered us out of the car. He immediately confiscated the video camera as well as my Canon A-1. The smug little man who first sounded the alarm was now taunting us, saying in broken English that we would all go to jail and that he would get our cameras. Again, we paid a fine and were allowed to continue on our way with the cameras.

With more than a week remaining until our departure, our dwindling finances were becoming critical. Between the gasoline, the cops, and the per-specimen fee for the animals, we were worried.

Limbé was only a short drive south from Buea, and we were back again in a hot, humid environment. We arrived in town just as some large, rickety boats full of illegally shipped gasoline were coming ashore from neighboring Nigeria. In addition to the gas boats, there were smaller vessels unloading fish. Among the more interesting species were five-to-six-foot sharks, giant eels more than five feet long, and toothy barracudalike fish with slender snouts and mouths full of long, razor-sharp teeth. I captured all these scenes on film, thanks to my hip shots and the recent "cold" I had contracted that caused me to "sneeze" incessantly.

After lunch we stopped briefly at the local zoo. The entry fee for residents was only ten cents; for foreign visitors, two dollars. If you wished to bring your camera with you, the fee increased to five dollars. Unlike zoos in the United States that prohibit feeding animals, this zoo encouraged it. With the country's poor economy and few foreign visitors, their financial situation was about as bad as our destitute group. After we paid the entrance fee, the guard asked if we would like to purchase some bananas to feed the monkeys. We obliged, and two dollars later we were loaded down with fruit.

This zoo was humble by any standards. There were just two long rows of wire cages, all exposed to the oppressive sun, and each containing a monkey and a branch but little else. As Joe walked by each cage, he presented the occupant with a ripe banana. When he got to the fourth cage, he was startled when one of the monkeys slipped out from between the bars, climbed up his leg, and grabbed several of the bananas from his hand. After consuming its food, the escaped mustached guenon (*Ceropithecus cephus*) proceeded from cage to cage, reached in, and stole the fruit from the other animals. Although the scene was amusing at the time, it certainly indicated a major problem.

Besides the main enclosures, there were only three other cages in the entire zoo. The manner in which the animals were paired seemed odd. In one cage were a scarlet macaw and an eagle; in another, an African civet (*Civettictis civetta*)—a spotted, mongooselike animal—and a West African dwarf crocodile (*Osteolaemus tetraspis*) shared space.

When I asked the keeper where the reptile house was, he took us into a small concrete room and pointed to a small wooden box resting on some bricks. "This is the reptile house?" I asked in disbelief.

"Well, we don't have many reptiles," the keeper replied. "In fact, this animal just came in this morning," he added. He carefully unlocked the box and took a step back. I looked at him for permission to open the container, and he nodded his approval. Inside was a gorgeous red, blue, green, and black, ten-inch-long juvenile rhinoceros viper *(Bitis nasicornis)*. We all stood around the box, impressed by the sight. I asked the caretaker if he would be willing to sell it, to which he replied that it was not for sale. I offered him thirty dollars for the snake, probably more than he made in a year. I could see he was tempted, but he explained that the owner of the zoo had already been notified the animal was there, and if it were to disappear, he would probably lose his job. I told him that I understood and asked him if he knew where the snake had come from. He said that a snake man had brought it in and that if we were interested, we could hire this man to take us to the place where he had collected it.

With that information, we waited around for a couple of hours until the snake man arrived. For a small fee, he offered to take us into the bush the next morning to hunt for snakes. He proclaimed himself to be "the master of all snake men in Cameroon." We were skeptical but agreed to meet him in the morning back at the zoo.

The next day he showed up wearing several necklaces and a small cloth pouch around his neck. He explained that these amulets possessed "magic powers" that would lead us to many snakes. We stared at him and smiled, not uttering a sound. We drove a few miles to a heavily forested area at the base of a small mountain. The snake man pointed to the top of the mountain and said that pygmy elephants live there, and if we wished, he would take us to see them. We told him that we were interested only in finding snakes, at which time he began chanting and sprinkling powder on the ground in front of him. With his eyes closed, he made a series of hand gestures to the sky, all the while chanting, singing, and waving the amulets that hung around his neck. We watched for almost thirty minutes, and still he made no effort to look for snakes. While he was performing his routine, Debbie and I slipped away to begin some "real" herping.

About an hour later, when a steady rain began to fall, we all retreated to a nearby shed. Sitting on the porch of this dilapidated hut was a native woman chopping up vegetables and paying little attention to our activities. She was dressed in a colorful native gown and was singing softly to herself. I desperately wanted to take a picture of her, but I knew she would never consent. So with Joe's help, I managed to get a few pictures of her by using my "sneeze" photography technique.

When the "snake man" finally caught up with us and had nothing to show, I asked him what the problem seemed to be. To this he responded, "Did you pray last night?"

"Pray?" I asked.

"Yes, did you pray to the Snake God?"

"No, I guess we forgot," I answered.

"Well, that explains it," he said. "Tonight you must pray to the Snake God, and tomorrow I will take you to find many snakes."

Despite my assurance to him that we would rendezvous again tomorrow morning, I had no intention of returning. With that we departed and drove several miles northeast to a neighboring town where we were told a "real" snake man lived.

Several locals who claimed to know him well directed us to the new snake man's house. They led us down a narrow corridor with broken glass bottles imbedded along the top of a six-foot-high wall, where we found a spacious backyard replete with banana trees and several small herbal gardens. In one corner of the yard was a tiny brick room no more than eight feet square. Inside, a man knelt on the floor with his head bowed and his eyes closed. It was difficult to see anything clearly, as the only light coming into the room was from the doorway and from two small, broken, and filthy windows. Much of that light, however, was being blocked by dozens of onlookers who peered through the glass. Without raising his head, the man (Sylvester) began to speak in English, although we soon discovered he was not talking to any of us but instead to the spirits.

"Oh, spirits from beyond this world, I need your help," Sylvester pleaded in a singsong voice. "Standing before me are several people who seek out my wisdom and help, and I need a sign that they are honest and trustworthy." In front of him on the ground lay half a dozen feathers embedded in what looked like Hershey kisses made of clay. He carefully placed the feathers flat on the ground, one on top of another, then placed a plastic bucket over them and began to sway back and forth, all the while speaking to the spirits.

"Give me a sign that these people are honest and true," he repeated. Then he quickly lifted the bucket, and to the crowd's amazement, all the feathers were standing upright. While any student of physics could clearly understand what had happened, the gathered masses were convinced that this man possessed special powers, and this bit of "magic" did much to reinforce Sylvester's control and power over them. He then looked up for the first time and spoke directly to us.

"The spirits have spoken," he said. "You are obviously good and honest people. How can I help you?"

"We are looking for snakes and other reptiles, and we were told that you know much about them," I replied. Upon hearing this, he stood up and reached for a suitcase hidden in the corner. After walking out of the room, he placed the suitcase on the ground in the middle of the back-yard.

By now, dozens of natives had gathered around to watch him as he opened the valise to reveal two large snakes. Immediately, the two black forest cobras reared up when exposed to the light and began to sway back and forth.

Sylvester started to reach into the suitcase to pull out one of the snakes. As his hand got closer to the cobras, both snakes raised up nearly two feet high and spread their hoods. Joe whispered, "Their mouths must be sewn shut."

As Sylvester slowly and cautiously reached for one of the snakes, it opened its mouth, preparing to bite.

When Sylvester picked up one of the serpents, we noticed that his left hand was missing both the index and middle fingers, and two of his other fingers were deformed and immobile. At that moment, Sylvester looked up at us and saw the shocked look on our faces.

"Yes, my hand," he said humbly. "It's from a bite I received many years ago from a large gaboon viper *(Bitis gabonica)*. The doctors wanted to remove my hand, but I didn't let them. I did, however, lose two of my fingers," he went on to explain. He then placed one cobra around his neck while he reached into the suitcase and removed the second one. With both snakes around his neck, he went into his lecture "routine" with all the onlookers watching his every move. He explained to the crowd what cobras eat, where they live, and how they mate. The information he gave was mostly correct, except for the statement that he alone could handle these snakes with complete immunity. As he spoke, one of the snakes crawled from his shoulders and disappeared under the house. Several of us quickly called this to his attention, but he merely responded: "It's all right, "Mary" likes to spend much of her time under the house. She'll come out shortly." Meanwhile, he put "John" back into the suitcase and returned it to the small brick room.

"So, you are interested in collecting snakes?" he asked as we sat in his modest home sipping cool drinks. "I can help you," he declared. Moments later, after Sylvester had retrieved "Mary" and placed her in the suitcase, we left his property and were on our way into the field to search for snakes. Since our vehicle was packed from top to bottom, we had no room for

Sylvester with his pet cobras, "John" and "Mary," in western Cameroon.

Sylvester. He said it was not a problem and that he would drive his own car. We were surprised that he could afford an automobile, so we asked him to explain how he had become so "wealthy" and famous.

Back in the early 1960s, he told us, the president of Cameroon had been giving a public speech, when the crowd started to become unruly. The police were unable to control the people and were fearful the crowd would swarm the president, causing him harm. At that time Sylvester was a young man and only recently had become interested in snakes. He had with him several live cobras, which he held in his hands, so he walked among the mob asking them to please disperse. In no time, the crowd parted, and this allowed the president to leave the area unharmed. As a reward for his assistance, the president bestowed on him the title "Snake Man of Cameroon," in addition to giving him a substantial amount of money.

With Joe in the passenger seat of his car and Sylvester's pet cobras in the trunk, the snake man led us out of town to search for snakes. His vehicle was equipped with a speaker on the roof, and while he drove, he loudly played a tape of the local music. Over this garbled and incoherent "noise," he used a microphone to speak to anyone within earshot.

"Yes, hello farmers, I have with me American researchers. Please stop me if you have any snakes in your possession. The people in the car behind me are looking for snakes. Please come forward if you have snakes in your yard, and we will catch them for you," he repeated again and again.

Several people did finally wave Sylvester down, only to sell him rats. Apparently, he drives around town on a regular basis, and the locals are more than willing to offer him a steady supply of rodents to feed "John" and "Mary." After purchasing each rodent, Sylvester would open his trunk and toss the helpless rat into the suitcase with the pair of cobras. After acquiring six rats, he no longer stopped to purchase food for his pets. The rats were actually African giant pouched rats (Cricetomys gambianus) and possessed the softest, most golden fur I had ever seen. As their name implies, they can store large quantities of food in their cheek pouches, much like chipmunks of North America.

When our "collecting" technique produced no results, Sylvester offered to stop at a nearby hotel where he knew someone who had recently captured a large snake. We learned that the hotel's owner, a friend of Sylvester's, was considered the leading herbalist in Cameroon. This information was of great interest to Joe, as his landlord in Houston was an amateur herbalist, and Joe was hoping to bring him samples of some local herbs, a poultice, or maybe even some kind of prescription written by the country's "leading" herbalist.

A security guard led us to a room devoid of all furniture except for a large ceramic bowl near the doorway and several burlap sacks piled in the far corner. The guard cautiously lifted the bags to reveal an eight-foot-long African rock python (Python sebae) curled up in a tight coil. Sylvester grabbed the snake, placed it around his neck, and walked outside, where onlookers shrieked and gasped. With a crowd of people now gathering around him, he went into lecture mode and began to talk about the snake draped over his shoulders. The snake seemed calm until Sylvester took a step forward. Now dangling just above the floor, the python struck Sylvester's sandaled foot and held on. I immediately raced over to help remove the python from his foot, but Sylvester did not seem at all concerned about being bitten and continued to lecture to the crowd. By the time I pulled the snake away, Sylvester was bleeding profusely from the numerous tooth marks around his ankle and heel. I wrapped my pillowcase around the wound to stop the bleeding, and ten minutes later Sylvester was back on his feet lecturing.

As the guard locked the snake back up in its room, he asked us if we were interested in taking the reptile with us to the United States. I appreciated his kind gesture, but explained that we did not have room in our luggage for an animal of that size. I also was not interested in acquiring a common snake that was emaciated and diseased, but I held my tongue and thanked him for his offer.

We then went to the main lobby, where we were told to wait until we could have an audience with the herbalist. A few minutes later, we were ushered into a large room adorned with animal skins and posters covering nearly every square inch of the walls. One of the skins was that of a ten-to-twelve-foot rock python (no doubt the last snake he tried unsuccessfully to give away), which hung over a poster showing the herbalist peering into a crystal ball that read, "Ask me a question, and I will answer it in less than 10 seconds." Beneath the poster sat the herbalist. He was a large man, dressed in a dark suit, and next to him was a guard who snapped to attention as we walked in. The herbalist did not stand when introduced to us but did offer to shake our hands. His English was weak, so Sylvester translated most of our conversation. We explained what we were doing in Cameroon, and he nodded in approval at our choice of guides. He then reached into a wooden box on a nearby table and began to roll a joint. This was no ordinary joint: it was the size of a small baseball bat and could easily have choked Cheech and Chong to death. He took several puffs from the "herbal cigarette" then tried to hand it to us. We all smiled politely, declining his offer. Now I understood why he was considered *the* herbalist of Cameroon.

Denis then asked whether we would all wait outside while Joe met in private with the herbalist. As we got to the door, Sylvester suddenly remembered that he had forgotten about his pets and raced to his car. "No, no, my children!" he shouted, when he opened his trunk to find both snakes dead. The temperature outside was in the upper nineties, and inside the car's trunk the temperature was well over one hundred degrees. The two cobras, unable to withstand such extreme heat, had quickly succumbed.

Sylvester was overwhelmed with emotion. "Paul, can you help me?" he asked, almost sobbing. "Can you help me by saving their bodies, so I will always have them with me?" he asked. Since each snake was over six feet long, I just did not have enough formalin with me to preserve them properly. I also lacked a container large enough to hold them. The best I could offer Sylvester was to skin the snakes and preserve the heads and tails. By then, he was so upset he could not even speak, so he nodded his approval to me. With Debbie's help, I prepared "John" and "Mary" and placed their bodies in a jar of preservative. Although Sylvester was extremely distraught, he was grateful for my help.

We now wondered why Joe was taking so long just to get an herb or a simple prescription. Several minutes later, Joe and Denis emerged from the hotel, whereupon Joe firmly instructed us to get into our vehicle, as we needed to leave immediately.

"What's up?" I asked Joe.

"Just drive!" he said.

En route back to Sylvester's home, I asked Joe several times what had happened, and each time Joe said he did not want to talk about it. It was not until Denis left us alone that Joe felt comfortable enough to explain.

Joe had asked Denis to request some kind of herb from the herbalist, to which Denis had replied that one does not ask for just any medicine; you have to state the problem then allow the herbalist to come up with a cure. Joe suggested that Denis say he had a cold, but Denis replied that any malady Joe might claim would have to be more substantial. Denis had then asked Joe a very personal question, one he said reflected a common problem among the local people.

"Joe, how many times a night do you *'perform'?"* Denis asked. Joe was very uncomfortable with this line of questioning and could not believe that he would be asked something so personal.

"Excuse me?" Joe said.

"You know, how many times a day . . ." Denis reiterated.

"Yes, I know what you're asking, but that's not a subject I'm comfortable discussing," Joe said sheepishly. Reluctantly, he finally said: "I guess on a good night, maybe twice, if I don't fall asleep first."

"Oh, no, you must not say that!" Denis said. "Tell the herbalist you can perform only five or six times a night, or he will think you are not a real man." All Joe could do was cough out an uncomfortable laugh and turn red. When the herbalist learned of Joe's "dilemma," he said that he wanted him to return alone that night, and he would make Joe into a whole man again. In response, Joe excused himself and retreated to the car, vowing to put as much distance as possible between himself and the "herbalist."

African burrowing
python *(Charina
reinhardtii)* from
southwestern
Cameroon.

Later that afternoon, Sylvester and several of his staff took us to a nearby
forest to look for snakes. Sylvester was still traumatized by the recent loss
of his cobras, and his participation in herping was clearly halfhearted.
Nonetheless, we did find an unusual toad buried under the leaf litter of a
giant fruit tree. It was extremely granular and had large spines on its head
and back. Its scientific name, *Bufo tuberosus,* reflected the spiny toad's
physical characteristics. One of Sylvester's assistants made the other significant find—a West African burrowing python, *Charina [Calabaria]
reinhardtii.* It was a stunning specimen, mostly dark brown with bright
orange spots scattered over its entire body. We have maintained other
individuals of this species at the Houston Zoo for years, but none had
had the bright orange markings of this snake.

When threatened, this small python demonstrates an unusual defense
tactic: it rolls up into a tight ball and tucks its head deep inside the coils.
At the same time, it raises its tail above its body and waves the tip of it,
which is rounded and looks exactly like the head. This behavior reduces
the chance that a predator will attack and injure the snake's more fragile
head. Although the permit fee for pythons was relatively high (twenty
dollars) and our money was disappearing rapidly, I definitely planned to
include this snake on my export list.

We could see that Sylvester was not enthusiastic about collecting with
us, so we thanked him for his help and continued on our way. Just as the
sun was setting, we came to the small village of Mutengene (pronounced
Moo-te-ha-nee). From the car, we saw a small stream that crossed under
the road—an excellent place to look for frogs. With darkness now upon
us, we walked along one of the stream banks, shining our flashlights on

the shrubs and rocks bordering the water. As we proceeded downstream, we detected a foul odor coming from the water. Careful inspection showed that the stench was caused by human waste deposited on the very rocks on which we were walking. Apparently the locals used this stream as a bathroom as well as a place to bathe and drink.

Finding only a couple of frogs on the overhanging foliage, we decided to drive to a more pleasant habitat. As we neared the bridge, we could see the silhouettes of people in the dim light, standing next to our vehicle and speaking in loud voices. Since there was some kind of commotion taking place, I suggested we leave as soon as possible. We certainly did not want to be stranded in town. By the time we reached our car, however, the mob had become much larger and more vocal. It now seemed that the people were shouting insults at us. As I unlocked the doors and started the car, I yelled for everyone to jump in. My suspicions that the crowd had grown hostile were confirmed when several people grabbed Denis and ordered us out of our locked car, while others rocked the car and pounded on the windows. Even Denis was shouting for us to exit the vehicle. Our group turned to me and asked what we should do. Given the circumstances, I said, "We need to do as they demand. Get out of the vehicle!" There was total chaos; we had no idea what was happening.

More than fifty people surrounded us and ushered us up the slope of a steep, muddy hill. With every step we took, their numbers grew, and their voices became louder and angrier. Halfway up the hill, we heard one man behind us ask another, "Did you bring the knives?" We were in serious trouble, and I had no idea why. Denis was several yards ahead of us, and I was unable to ask him what was going on. At this point, the local men grabbed each of us by the arms and roughly shook us. I reached over to Debbie, wrapped my arm around her to protect her, and whispered to her that if we got out of this alive, I would take it as a sign that we should get married. As I reflect on it now, my statement seems overly dramatic, but I was sincere at the time, and given the circumstances, I felt it was appropriate.

With the mob all around us, we were forced into a small house along the edge of the hill. An elderly couple was sitting on a couch, watching television. I wish I had paid more attention to what they were watching, but at the time I was too preoccupied with trying to stay alive. After turning off the television, the man stood up and demanded to know what was going on.

"Bombs. They were planting bombs in our river, chief," one of the men screamed.

"Yes, I too saw them setting off bombs down by the water," another man chimed in. I was thinking to myself that these people had completely lost their minds. Why would they think we were planting bombs in their stream? Then it dawned on me. They had seen us using our camera flash units to take pictures of frogs and assumed we were detonating explosives. Finally, I knew what was going on. Our only chance of escaping this predicament hinged on the chief being able to calm the mob and allow us to explain our side of the story.

Looking over the heads of the men around him, the chief asked who saw us planting bombs.

"I did!" said the head vigilante from the back of the room.

"Who is speaking? What is your name?" the chief demanded. The man's response was inaudible. "Please be quiet!" the chief shouted to everyone. "I cannot hear his name." Again, the man repeated his name in a soft tone, and once more the chief was unable to understand him. Passing a pencil and a piece of paper towards the rear of the room, the chief asked the man to write down his name.

With his head hung low, the man whispered back to the chief that he did not know how to write. For a brief moment, I felt sorry for him. I realized that for years I had taken reading and writing for granted, while many people throughout the world—including this man—had not mastered such skills. But my thoughts were interrupted by Denis's loud shriek:

"What? *This* is the head vigilante, the strongest among you, the man responsible for everyone's safety, the one that can't even write his own name?" he scolded. Debbie, Joe, and Mike glanced over to me, each sporting an expression of absolute terror. None of us spoke, although we were certain we were all now doomed. What was Denis thinking? Was this some kind of carefully calculated tactic that would give us the upper hand? Joe touched Denis on the hand, put his finger up to his mouth, and shook his head almost imperceptibly as if to say, "Are you insane; keep your mouth shut." Fortunately, a few of the men in the room seemed amused at this gesture and nodded in agreement with Denis's attack.

To our surprise and relief, the chief shouted to the angry crowd, "Everyone, please be quiet so I can talk to these people." While the crowd fell silent, the chief asked for any papers we had to indicate what we were doing in this area. With all eyes on me, I slowly reached into my camera vest and produced our research proposal as well as copies of our passports. The tension of the moment was palpable; I could feel my heart pounding through my chest, temples, and throat. Adding to the anxiety of the moment was the oppressive heat, coupled with the body heat of more than sixty people crammed into the tiny dwelling. As I unfolded the crumpled papers, several large beads of sweat poured from my forehead and beard onto the documents. Wiping the droplets from the pages, I could not calm my trembling hands.

The chief briefly looked over the documents, then addressed the crowd: "These are not terrorists," he began. "These are Americans; they are our friends! They are not planting bombs; they are here doing research." From the back of the packed room we could occasionally hear angry voices rising in protest to what the chief was saying. "I hear you in the back, cursing and challenging me," he said. "I know what you are saying behind my back. I know that many of you disagree with me, but I am *still* the head of this village, and you *will* do as I say. Perhaps someday, by the grace of God, one of your children may be lucky enough to visit America. Then you will wish you had gotten to know these people better, so they might help you as they have asked us to help them."

The speech was moving and powerful, but I could not help thinking that although we might have temporarily escaped the townpeople's wrath, our vehicle was already in a thousand little pieces. When I brought up the subject of our car, the chief assured me that no harm would come to it.

Despite the chief's advanced age (he was easily in his seventies) and gentle demeanor, the hostile crowd obeyed him and began to disband. He was preparing to let us go when the younger of his two wives whispered something in his ear. She suggested that we be taken to a nearby police station to have our story checked out by the authorities. Because the local officials are so easily bribed (this includes murder and other such serious crimes), we had not initially been taken to the police. The natives had feared we would simply buy our way out of the "crime" and go free. This is why we were first taken to the village chief, so that permission to have us killed might be granted. The entire ordeal was extremely unnerving, and we were badly shaken by the experience.

Since none of the local people had a vehicle, we had to wait for a taxi so that the town's "vigilantes," as they called themselves, could escort us to the police station. Three men piled into the cab, while two others squeezed into our vehicle—lest we try to escape. Despite the cramped conditions, I was relieved that our car was intact and undamaged.

The scene at the police station was like something out of an old movie. At the back of the small, dilapidated building was a card table with a bare, dim bulb dangling above it. Sitting around the table were four policemen in the midst of a card game, each smoking a cigarette. As we approached, one of the vigilantes began to speak, but before he could finish his sentence, the head of police roughly interrupted him and demanded to see our papers. I handed him our research proposal as well as copies of our passports.

"What seems to be the problem?" he asked in an irritated tone.

"We were afraid that these people were terrorists," the head vigilante replied in an almost inaudible voice.

"Terrorists!?" the policeman shouted back. "These are Americans, not terrorists."

I was thankful that many people, including these policemen, did not consider Americans terrorists.

"Let them go!" the police chief commanded. And with that, we were finally free. The vigilantes then surprised us by shaking our hands and offering to take us out into the bush to search for frogs. We thanked them politely, but declined their invitation.

At this point, we were far too frazzled to camp out. Instead, we found a hotel (a fair distance away) and spent the night recounting the recent traumatic events until we could discuss them no longer.

The following morning, Mike seemed agitated and distant. He wanted to return to Mutengene and talk to the chief. Even Denis, who to my surprise once lived in Mutengene, advised against this, but Mike said he was going back with or without us and asked Denis to take him.

Minutes later, they headed south to Mutengene. It was not until much later that I discovered the reason for Mike's actions. He confided to me that he had felt somewhat intimidated by the entire episode and sought to regain his self-esteem by returning to the town and confronting his aggressors.

By midafternoon, they finally returned. Mike was smiling and seemed back to his usual self. He told us that the chief had actually expected us to return and was so impressed when Mike showed up, he made him an honorary village leader. He showed Mike pictures of his daughter, who is in the States, as well as of his family in Cameroon. The villagers served Denis and him lunch, and then the three of them talked for hours. "I knew it was the right thing to do," Mike said.

With Mike feeling better and the rest of us calm again, we began our trek back to Douala. Our journey took us through the center of Mutengene, and with my camera pointed out of the car window, I employed my machine-gun photography technique and captured on film the place where we nearly met our end.

With our funds now almost gone, we were forced to do the unthinkable—purchase gasoline from roadside vendors. Although I would not want to put that gas into my own car, it did save us enough money to afford to eat on the way back.

Returning the car to the rental agency, we settled our staggering bill of forty-three hundred dollars for the three weeks and the additional mileage. For that kind of money, we could have purchased the vehicle outright then sold it for a profit. At this point we had just enough money to cover the permit fee and little else. With my few remaining dollars, I purchased the only souvenir of the trip—a beautiful handmade wooden mask with images of chameleons and frogs outlined on it.

It was time now to visit the permit office, the most nerve-racking task of these expeditions. In keeping with Cameroonian tradition, I had problems from the onset. First, I was told that the man in charge of issuing permits would not be in the office until the following week. Then I was told the fee for the specimens was more than indicated on the "tariff" sheet. I finally found someone who could write up the export permit, but then I was told it would take three weeks. Only after handing over my last dollar to the clerk was I assured that the permit would be ready in a few hours.

When I returned to pick up the permit later in the day, the clerk was still preparing the document. We made brief eye contact, and I smiled at him as I walked over to his desk to check on his progress. What I read on the paper in the typewriter upset me greatly. Any animals of which we had collected more than one species were lumped together as a group. This meant that the two species of toads were listed as *Bufo* sp., the two chameleon species as *Chamaeleo* sp., and so forth.

I immediately interrupted the gentleman to point out this serious error, but he did not even look up when he said, "It has to be this way, or the magistrate won't sign it."

"I'm sorry," I said, "I don't understand."

"If the document is more than one page long, the head of the wildlife division will not sign it," he said in an irritated voice.

"I understand, but if I arrive in the United States without the proper documents, all my specimens will be confiscated," I pleaded.

For the first time since my arrival, he looked directly at me, pushed back his chair, and said in a hostile tone, "Do you, or do you not, want this permit?" I realized that I would not be able to convince him to change his mind, and I also sensed that I was very close to losing the permit entirely. All I could do was to accept the document as prepared and hope that the wildlife officials in the United States would be more understanding. After affixing the CITES stamps and securing the magistrate's signature on the permit, I left the building.

The trip was winding down to the last few hours, and we had one more unpleasant task at hand—saying good-bye to our newfound friend and guide, Denis. He had come through for us time and time again, whether it was bailing us out of jail, translating our needs to the locals, or just being available to talk to. When it came time to pay him for his services, we felt very uncomfortable, for with all of our other unexpected expenses, we could afford to give him only a tiny fraction of what he deserved. To make up for part of the cash deficiency, we left him most of our camping equipment, extra clothes and shoes, snacks, flashlights, and anything else we could spare.

Before boarding the van to the airport, I wanted to provide our prize catch, the West African burrowing python, with a final drink of water. I did not want to risk the snake's injury or death by putting it in the cargo hold of the aircraft with the other specimens, so I planned on keeping it hidden in one of my many vest pockets. But when I removed the snake from the cloth bag, I discovered that it was dead. I was crestfallen. The catch of the trip, and it was dead. What a fitting end to an altogether miserable trip. I quickly preserved the python and we were on our way.

As we approached the airport terminal, Denis warned us that the guards there were notorious for opening bags during routine inspections and taking whatever they wanted. So, before arriving, we made sure all of our belongings were secured and locked.

At the airport, porters vying to carry our bags to the departure gate mobbed us. Having no money to pay them, we explained that we did not need their services. This did not deter the handlers, and several of them fought among themselves for the opportunity to transport our bags. Eventually, Denis was able to convince them that we had absolutely no money and that we could not pay for their assistance. We finally made our way to the departure lounge that we shared with fifty or sixty other passengers, all of them white, and all of them complaining to each other about the terrible experiences they had endured in Cameroon. We sat in silence and smiled at each other, thankful just to be alive.

After many hours in the air, we finally touched down in New York. I first declared the reptiles and amphibians to a customs agent, then immediately sought out a U.S. Fish and Wildlife officer to help me with the appropriate paperwork. I held my breath as the wildlife agent went through each container to be sure that all the animals were properly listed on the CITES export document. Then, as I predicted, the worst happened.

"Mr. Freed, what is *Chamaeleo* sp.?" the agent asked.

"That represents two species of chameleons: *Chamaeleo montium* and *Chamaeleo cristatus*," I said anxiously.

"Yes, but it doesn't state that on the permit. It just says, '*Chamaeleo* sp.,'" she reiterated.

"I know, but the permit office in Cameroon refused to list each species separately due to space limitations," I responded.

"Well, then how do I know which species you are importing?" she continued.

"I'm telling you which species," I said, "*C. montium* and *C. cristatus.*"

"But it doesn't say that on the permit," she said impatiently. I told her that all chameleon species are Appendix II (not endangered) and that I had all the relevant CITES stamps and permits.

"OK, what is *Bufo* sp.?" she asked. I grinned, lowered my head, and shook it from side to side.

"Again, the permit office condensed all the same genera into one entry," I stated.

"But how do I know what species you are importing?" she repeated.

"I'm telling you which species: *Bufo maculatus* and *Bufo tuberosus.*"

"But it doesn't say that on your permit," she said.

I felt as though I were in the middle of an Abbott and Costello routine. Although I had anticipated this happening, I thought that I would certainly be able to convince the authorities that I was not trying to deceive them by pulling some sort of con game. By now, however, I was exasperated and extremely irritated, so I walked away from the agent to avoid becoming openly hostile. She told me to wait while she called her supervisor for another opinion. Twenty minutes later, she returned and informed me that she was seizing the entire shipment as instructed by her superiors. After a year of preparation, a month in hell, and an expense of over ten thousand dollars—now all my specimens were to be confiscated? I was livid. The agent gave me the name of her supervisor in Washington and suggested I contact him if I had a problem. In the meantime, all the live herps would be deposited at the Bronx Zoo until further notice.

The day after I returned to Houston, I was on the telephone to officials in Washington trying to clear up this nightmare. It took me nearly five months of negotiating, but in the end I was victorious; all my specimens were returned to me. As I had expected, a number of them had died during that time, but I was pleased to have been vindicated by the Washington Bureau and happy to have put the entire episode of Cameroon behind me. However, the drama of Cameroon did not end there.

• •

The setting was idyllic. A wall of greenery surrounded us. Every tree was festooned with mosses, orchids, and bromeliads of countless varieties. The aroma of the blooming flowers was intoxicating. The early morning air was cool, and a damp mist blanketed the landscape. A light rain had been falling, making the ground slick and muddy. In the distance, parrots squawked noisily while dozens of hummingbirds filled the skies around us. It was a magical day.

We walked up the steep hill, each of us slipping and falling on the water-soaked earth. No one cared; we were all glad just to be here, to be part of the celebration. After nearly an hour, we reached our destination. On a clear day here, you could see from one end of the world to the other. Today, however, our gaze stopped on each other. While we stood in a small clearing, our friends held up sheets and towels to shield us from the elements as we shed our soiled, wet clothes and metamorphosed into two well-groomed, more handsome creatures.

Her long white gown danced in the breeze just above the shallow and turbid puddles. Nestled in her perfectly coifed hair was a native orchid, which accentuated her pale blue eyes. She was absolutely stunning.

With our friends surrounding us in this breathtaking backdrop, we exchanged vows in a simple but significant ceremony. Debbie and I were now husband and wife. Given our lifestyle of travel and adventure, this setting was a most appropriate one at which to begin our lives as one—the Monteverde Cloud Forest Reserve of Costa Rica.

As I scanned the wedding party, my mind wandered to the events that had brought me to this time and place—events that had dramatically shaped my life—foremost being that fateful trip to Cameroon.

Epilogue

AS A RESULT OF MY RESEARCH expeditions, more than one hundred new species of parasites have been described. Along with finding these new life-forms, I have found new life philosophies. I have noticed a dramatic transition in my thinking concerning living creatures. My research started as I began my new career in a zoological setting, leading me away from the doctrines of a strict museum philosophy. Zoo people are of a very different breed. For the most part, they are against any action or behavior that may cause injury or death to their charges. The whole concept of zoos is, of course, predicated upon displaying healthy animals for education, wildlife conservation, and public enjoyment. At the beginning of my zoo experiences, immediately following my museum indoctrination, I was almost mechanical in my approach to living animals. They were still just "specimens" to me, something that evoked no compassion or emotional attachment. And despite their significance and interconnectedness to all living things, these animals were merely objects that I would eventually just preserve. It did not matter whether they were the rarest, most beautiful, or even the last of their kind; I had no qualms about preserving them. Today, however, that has all changed. While I still see the need for and importance of museum collections, I no longer feel compelled to be the one to bolster their numbers. As a result of this evolution, I have ceased collecting and preserving animals, choosing instead to concentrate on observing, photographing, and enjoying them in the wild.

ISBN 1-58544-271-2